Scripture 101
An Intro to Reading the Bible

WILLIAM J. PARKER, C.Ss.R.

Liguori
LIGUORI, MISSOURI

Imprimi Potest:
Thomas D. Picton, C.Ss.R.
Provincial, Denver Province
The Redemptorists

Published by Liguori Publications
Liguori, Missouri
To order, call 800-325-9521
www.liguori.org

© 2009, William J. Parker, C.Ss.R.

Library of Congress Cataloging-in-Publication Data

Parker, William J., C. Ss. R.
   Scripture 101: an intro to reading the Bible / William J. Parker—
1st ed.
      p. cm.
   ISBN 978-0-7648-1700-7
   1. Bible—Introductions. I. Title.
   BS475.3.P36 2009
   220.6'1—dc22

2008050907

Liguori Publications, a nonprofit corporation, is an apostolate of the Redemptorists. To learn more about the Redemptorists, visit Redemptorists.com.

Printed in the United States of America
13 12 11 10 09   5 4 3 2 1
First edition

CONTENTS

PART THREE: READING THE NEW TESTAMENT

Introduction

The Second Vatican Council called attention to the need for the Bible in every day Catholic living. Catholics responded to the call. After Vatican II, new Catholic translations of the Bible appeared, and study groups were popular in parishes; some Catholic churches even held "Bible vigils" during Advent and Lent. But much of that initial fervor quieted. People moved on, with or without their Bibles. Today, many obstacles to concentrated Bible study exist. For most adults, time is a factor; their lives are too crowded as is. Some shy away from joining a Bible study group for fear it will be "hijacked" by some religious zealot in the group. Others feel they get their Bible "fill" at the homily during Sunday Mass. Whatever the reason, for many Catholics, the Bible is a closed book even before they open it.

If the Bible is really God's Word, then shouldn't it be easy to understand or, at least, to read? Neither is the case. Even though we might have many favorite passages, the language and the images behind those words may be foreign to us. And even if I work through the process of trying to understand a biblical book, I may not really believe that it has something to say to me today. Do Paul and his convoluted arguments about righteousness make sense in my world? Is Moses anything more than a celluloid figure in a biblical epic that looks and sounds an awful lot like the late Charlton Heston?

I believe that our preconceptions about the Bible are the biggest blocks to our understanding. Preconceptions are funny things; we all have them but, for the most part, we don't realize how they affect the way we see the world around us. One of the most common preconceptions about the Bible is that it is a historical record of all that happened from the time God created the world until the time shortly after Jesus Christ's ascension into heaven. While the Bible contains much that is historical, it is not history the way we understand it today. Another major assumption is that every word in the Bible must be taken literally, even though much of what the Bible says clashes with modern day science and historical investigations. Finally I believe that many of us intuitively turn to the Bible because we expect it to help us solve our personal problems and provide answers to our questions.

Over the last thirty-five years, I have had the privilege and opportunity to study the Bible and teach it in college universities, seminaries, and parish Bible study groups. Though my training was in the rigorous academic world of The Catholic University of America, my heart was always drawn to a more pastoral approach. Early on I decided I wanted to be a bridge between the very specialized research of the academics and the needs of ordinary people who want to understand how God's Word affects their attitudes and choices. This book is part of that attempt to bridge.

Scripture 101 does not explain all the difficult passages in the Bible; rather it is intended for people who would like to read the Bible with a little more understanding or to study it by themselves or in a group. When I am in unfamiliar territory, like an art museum or a foreign country, I like to have a guidebook along. It provides enough background to help me know what to look for and thus appreciate the experience. That is what I hope the chapters in this book will do for those interested in the Bible.

The book is divided into three parts. A general section entitled "Before Beginning" looks at some of the usual preconceptions we have about the Bible itself. The chapters in this part should be read first since the rest of the book builds upon them. The next two sections deal with the Old and New Testaments respectively. The chapters in these sections can be read in any order depending on one's interests, or simply read in the sequence in which they appear. All of the chapters include further resources for study and some questions for reflection or to begin a discussion with others.

Listening to the Word of God is not a simple task, nor should it be lest we trivialize it; however, it is not impossible either. This book will guide you through some of the questions that often bring people to a grinding halt in their journey into the Bible. Along the way, I will offer some encouraging insights into these sacred texts that will challenge you and hopefully encourage your own personal study.

PART ONE

Before Beginning

CHAPTER 1

How the Bible Came to Be

A traveling businessman noticed the passenger seated next to him on a plane reading the Bible. During the flight, the two began talking. The businessman asked the gentleman which translation of the Bible he preferred. The passenger said he read the King James version because the lofty phrasing helped him feel closer to God. The businessman said that he preferred his grandmother's translation. The other man, familiar with many Bible translations, had never heard of a version translated by a grandmother, so he asked about it. The businessman replied, "Oh, her work was never put in writing; she translated the Bible into action every day of her life."

The Bible is both a written document and, at the same time, the inspired Word of God. As a written document, the Bible has been translated into countless languages to be read and studied by people in every culture and country. But how did this written document we call the Bible come to exist in the first place?

The word *bible* comes from the Greek word, *biblia*, which means "a collection of books." We tend to think of the Bible as one book written by God with a consistent message; however, the Bible is not just one book but rather a library of books. Like books in any library, the books of the Bible were written at different times by many different individuals. Over time they were gathered into larger collections like the Torah, the Prophets, and the Writings.

AN ORAL TRADITION

Before the Bible was put into written form, all the stories, events, and messages in the Old Testament were told and retold and handed on from one generation to the next. This oral tradition circulated in family groups, in local areas, and often in worship settings. The Gospels originated in the same manner. The stories were told and retold by apostles and missionary preachers while celebrating the Eucharist in the homes of the first Christians.

In the Old Testament, this oral tradition consisted of stories about important figures in a family or tribe (Abraham, Moses, Samuel, David, and so forth). It also consisted of wise advice from a parent to a child in the form of proverbs and rules. Some stories explained how locations and people got their names and included tales about mysterious appearances of God to special individuals. Around 1000 BCE when David became king, Israel emerged as an important player on the world stage. As a young nation, Israel developed a new government and the bureaucracy to go with it. Scribes with narrative and poetic skills began to weave these oral traditions into written form. This process was just the beginning. It would be another eight hundred years before the Jews had a collection of scrolls containing most of the books in their Bible.

The Pentateuch (Genesis, Exodus, Leviticus, Numbers, and Deuteronomy) was probably written by four different authors, though this matter is still debated by scholars. Each author collected the oral traditions available in his locale at the time, telling the story of how Israel came to be the Chosen People of God, each from his own perspective. One author, whom scholars call "J," describes God in very human terms to show how accessible God is in people's lives. Another, called "E," emphasizes the distance between God and humans to underscore the need for a reverential fear or awe of the Lord. A third author, identified as "P," deals mainly with God's gift of law so that humans will be able to live in union with God. The final author, "D," is responsible for the great sermons in Deuteronomy, in which Moses reminds the Chosen People of the accountability of God's love.

Scholars believe that in the fifth century BCE, these four documents were edited and combined to tell one complete story of how Israel came to be. The story was then copied onto five scrolls, which became the Torah, or "the Law," the most sacred collection of texts of the Jewish people. We might say that the Bible was born at this point. It didn't take long for the Bible to grow after that. The development of the other books in the Old Testament began, like the Torah, as oral traditions that were preserved by disciples and later put into writing.

THE WRITING PROPHETS

The biblical prophets appeared on the scene during the reigns of various kings in Israel's history. This appearance was not a coincidence. In God's plan, the kings were to shepherd the people and exemplify obedience to the covenant with God. In reality, the kings became despotic, acting like gods themselves. The prophets came to speak God's words directly to the people and to challenge the kings for their failure to do so. Their message reiterated that of Deuteronomy; God held the Chosen People accountable for their covenant violations.

At first these proclamations were preserved in memory by disciples of the prophets. When the Israelite kingdoms fell as the prophets said they would, these words were put into writing so that future generations might not make the same mistake earlier generations had made. By the third century BCE, the prophets' words were collected into four scrolls, one for each of the major prophets (Isaiah, Jeremiah, and Ezekiel) and a single scroll to hold the sayings of twelve of the less verbose "minor" prophets.

The remaining books of the Old Testament came to exist in a similar fashion, though the actual date that the documents were written is almost impossible to know. All that can legitimately be said is that Josephus, a Jewish historian in the first century CE, acknowledged a list of twenty-two sacred books as part of the Jewish canon. Not every Jewish group agreed with that list. The Jews at Qumran had a different list of sacred books, and the Greek-speaking Jews in Egypt had yet another list of sacred writings. Not until the second century CE would the Jews agree on a final list of twenty-four books, which they grouped into three divisions: the Law, the Prophets, and the Writings.

The New Testament came to be written in a similar process. The letters of Paul were probably the first writings of the New Testament. After Jesus' death and resurrection, his disciples certainly proclaimed the "Good News," that is, the Gospel. But as communities of believers began to grow, and questions arose about what it means to be a disciple of Christ, the need for encouragement and correction was most urgent. The letters of Paul, and presumably those of other apostles, were written to address the specific needs of particular communities.

GOSPEL BEGINNINGS

While the letters of Paul and others gave the early Christian communities some direction, the Gospels are what brought them together. The word *gospel* means "preached or proclaimed good news." It is not just a happy story; rather it is a message that others hear and respond to as good news in their lives. Let me give you an example.

When I was teaching in the seminary many years ago, our major superior from Rome visited at the time of the students' final exams in May. He announced at lunch that he was canceling all final exams. The students' first reaction was stunned silence; they could not believe their ears. Then the dining room erupted in applause, laughter, shouts of joy, and songs. They had heard *good news* and they were responding to it. The employees working in the kitchen had also heard the announcement, but the message was not "good news" for them. Though they might have been happy for the students, they did not feel a need to respond in the same way.

That example underscores what gospel really means. It is a message that is proclaimed and heard by others as good news. The Gospels are not biographies as we understand that word today, though the stories about Jesus are told in some kind of chronological order. It is the preaching of Jesus and the message of salvation for all that is the "Good News." When the disciples first saw the risen Jesus, they were initially stunned and then overwhelmed with joy. The Gospels began at that point.

Those first disciples went far and wide spreading the Good News. They would meet in houses and in the town centers, wherever they could gather a group of people and tell them about Jesus. They would recall his teaching and tell about events in his life that exemplified his message. In time, however, the apostles were being killed, so different authors in various communities began to gather these stories and teachings together into written form. Each evangelist, or Gospel writer, used the traditions that circulated in his locale and crafted the Good News for his own audience.

While many people think of the Gospels as biographies, it is helpful to consider them portraits of Christ, painted by great artists, using words instead of oils. While a photograph reflects what the camera lens catches at a specific moment in time, a painting is quite different. An artist may choose to paint the same image captured in a photograph, but an artist has choices in color, texture, perspective, and other techniques to give an interpretation of the image for the viewer.

This analogy may help us understand why there are four Gospels. The Gospels are not four reprints of a photograph of Christ. If we consider the Gospels to be biographies of Christ, then, like photographs, we expect the reprints to match. But the Gospels do not agree on many basic points in the life of Christ. However, if the purpose of the Gospels is to proclaim a message demanding a response, then each Gospel paints a different picture that evokes a different response from a particular Christian community.

BIBLICAL PORTRAITS

For example, Mark's portrait of Jesus emphasizes the cross and the sufferings of Jesus. But the most striking element in this painting is the difficulty the disciples have understanding who Jesus is. At the same time, today's reader of the Gospel knows right from the start what the disciples struggled to understand. When we are continually baffled by suffering in our lives, we recognize the difficulty of understanding who Jesus is. Matthew, on the other hand, pictures Jesus as the perfect Israelite who continues to challenge his Jewish audience to reexamine their obstinate refusal to accept Jesus as the Messiah. Matthew's portrait challenges believers to accept a Messiah quite different from the one expected. Luke's Gospel accentuates Jesus' compassion for the outcasts of society and challenges "would be" disciples to get beyond a mindset that excludes people from God's salvation. Finally, John paints a picture of a divine Jesus united with the Father, but who has not left us orphans. He is in our midst right now. Jesus challenges his disciples to live in truth and to humbly serve one another.

Many other gospels existed in the early Christian church, such as the Gospel of Peter and that of Mary Magdalene. Many other letters from apostolic writers like Barnabas and Clement circulated around the early Christian communities. But these works never became part of the New Testament. For centuries, there would be a debate about which books belonged in the New Testament. Not until 397, at the Council of Carthage, did the churches in the East and the West agree on the twenty-seven books that make up the New Testament today.

CONCLUSION

The Scriptures evolved over a long period of time spanning countless generations. The stories that were told, remembered, handed on, and finally written down were never meant to be archives researched by historians of another time. They do contain a great deal of material that is important in any historical research, but they have a much larger purpose. The stories of the Bible were told and retold because they are God's Word requiring a response from those who hear or read them. Whether the stories were told by an elder sitting around a fire with a family eager to hear about their ancestor, David, or are read today by someone sitting in his or her favorite easy chair before the fireplace, the demand is still the same. Do we believe what we have just heard and read, and does that message make any difference in our life?

DISCUSSION QUESTIONS

1. *How does the image of the Bible as a library of books help or hinder your understanding of Scripture?*
2. *If the Bible began as stories passed on from one generation to the next, wouldn't that process affect the accuracy of the details in the Bible?*
3. *Is there an oral tradition in your own family that has not yet been written down but gets retold whenever your family gets together?*
4. *What is the difference between the major and minor prophets?*
5. *The author describes a gospel as a "proclamation of good news" and not a "biography" or a "life of Christ." What is the difference? Why is this important to know when reading the Gospels?*
6. *Why do we have four Gospels? Wouldn't one be enough?*

FURTHER READING

Brettler, Marc Z. *How to Read the Bible*. New York: Jewish Publication Society of America, 2005.

Friedman, Richard Elliott. *Who Wrote the Bible?* San Francisco: HarperSanFrancisco, 1997.

Lienhard, Joseph T. *The Bible, the Church, and Authority: The Canon of the Christian Bible in History and Theology*. Collegeville, MN: Liturgical Press, 1995.

Miller, John W. *The Origins of the Bible: Rethinking Canon History*. Mahwah, N.J.: Paulist Press, 1994.

Witherup, Ronald D. *The Bible Companion: A Handbook for Beginners*. New York: The Crossroad Publishing Company, 1998.

CHAPTER 2
Understanding Inspiration: How the Bible Was Written

Christians and Jews agree that the Bible is God's Word; how they understand what that means is another story. Over the centuries different explanations of inspiration have resulted in different ways to interpret that Word. Focusing on two explanations at opposite ends of the spectrum can help us find a middle ground.

The most common misunderstanding of biblical inspiration is sometimes referred to as the dictation theory. According to this theory, God spoke the words of Scripture, and the human author wrote them down like a secretary taking dictation. Caravaggio, an Italian painter in the late-sixteenth century, created a painting of Saint Matthew for a church in Rome. Caravaggio's painting illustrates this common misunderstanding of inspiration as dictation. In the painting, Saint Matthew is anxiously writing down everything an angel hovering over his shoulder tells him.

Another less common but equally one-sided view of inspiration depicts the human author as totally responsible for the Scriptures. In this view, the human author came up with the idea and wrote it down. God liked what the human author wrote and claimed it as inspired. This approach, called the subsequent approbation theory, simply means that God approved what was written after the fact. A similar process takes place today when the president of the United States gives a speech. One or more writers prepare drafts of the speech, and the president selects the parts he likes, which then become his speech. History will remember this speech as given by the president; the actual speechwriters may never be known by name.

The problem with both of these theories is the misplaced emphasis on who is the real author. In the dictation theory, all the emphasis is on God as the author. The human being plays no significant role except to be the channel by which God's words got onto the scroll or papyrus. In the subsequent approbation theory, the emphasis is solely upon the human author. God did not really have a hand in the writing, but simply approved what was written after the fact. In the course of tradition, the Catholic Church rejected both theories.

We might be tempted to think of biblical inspiration as a delicate balance between God and the human author, but that would not reflect the deeper mystery that the Catholic teaching tries to preserve. Inspiration as a balance implies that two elements have their own separate roles to play, like two weights on a scale. But with biblical inspiration, *both* God *and* the human person are the author. If we do not keep the mystery clearly in mind, we tend to focus on one aspect of this mystery, usually the divine, and ignore the other, the human. It is not an easy task to reverence this mystery when our practical side wants to know how it works.

In many ways this mystery of the divine/human authorship of the Bible is similar to the mystery of the Incarnation, which teaches that Jesus Christ is both God and man. Christians believe in the Incarnation, but may put greater emphasis on one aspect over the other. Some want to emphasize the divine powers that Jesus possessed; others want to focus on his human limitations. Both aspects of the mystery of the Incarnation must be held together.

WHAT IS INSPIRATION?

The Catholic Church has wrestled with this balance of biblical inspiration for centuries. The clearest statement of the Catholic Church's teaching on inspiration is found in the Dogmatic Constitution on Divine Revelation (*Dei verbum*), promulgated in 1965 at the conclusion of the Second Vatican Council. The statement was a summary of the Church's pronouncements going back to the Council of Trent, the First Vatican Council, and the encyclicals of two popes: *Providentissimus Deus* in 1893 (Pope Leo XIII) and *Divino Afflante Spiritu* in 1943 (Pope Pius XII).

In the Dogmatic Constitution on Divine Revelation, we find the classic definition of inspiration: "In composing the sacred books, God chose men and while employed by Him they made use of their powers and abilities, so that with Him acting in them and through them, they, as true authors, consigned to writing everything and only those things which He wanted" (*DV* 11). This official teaching sounds convoluted, but it was carefully crafted over the centuries to avoid misunderstanding. It can be restated in a simpler way: the Bible is God's Word in human words. Both God and human beings are the authors of the books of the Bible. The human author wrote freely as any human author would, in the style and idiom of his or her own time, using literary forms and images that would be familiar to the audience of that time. Yet all the while the human author was freely writing, he or she was writing only what God wanted written and not one word more or less.

To understand what God is saying in the Bible, we have to take seriously what the human author actually wrote down on parchment or papyrus. That human author wrote in a language and in a culture vastly different than ours, using literary forms that we may be unfamiliar with. Once again the Dogmatic Constitution on Divine Revelation outlines the task that biblical interpreters should undertake: "...[T]he interpreter of sacred Scripture, in order to see clearly what God wanted to communicate to us, should carefully investigate what meaning the sacred writers really intended, and what God wanted to manifest by means of their words" (*DV* 12). In other words, we cannot hope to truly understand what God is saying if we don't understand what the human author intended to communicate.

WHAT IS THE POINT?

If we accept the Catholic teaching on biblical inspiration, then we cannot just interpret the Scriptures literally. This is the mistake of biblical fundamentalists, who put all their focus on the divine aspect of inspiration. A good Catholic understanding of inspiration must keep both the divine and the human author together. If we want to understand what God is saying in the Bible, then we have to pay attention to the human author. This human author is the only way we have of getting to God's Word.

For the ordinary Catholic, then, three areas must be considered when studying any book of the Bible. First, we must consider the time frame in which the human author wrote. The Bible was produced over a long period of time: at least twelve hundred years. When reading or studying a particular book of the Bible, we need to ask ourselves what was happening at the time the biblical author was writing this particular book. What did the world look like from the biblical author's viewpoint? A second area of consideration must be the audience for whom the authors wrote. Where did they live? What kind of culture and society did they form? What were their customs? What questions did they have? Finally, what form(s) of writing did the biblical author employ to convey his or her message? This last point is perhaps the most important.

Most of us instinctively understand the forms used in written communication today. For example, in reading a newspaper, we know the difference between a news item and an advertisement.

Likewise we expect a news article to contain verifiable facts and an editorial to express opinion. Each of these forms (a news story, an editorial, and an advertisement) can appear in a *single* newspaper. It is the same in the Bible. One or several different literary forms may appear in a particular biblical book. However, modern readers often don't recognize the different forms or notice the shift from one form to another within a biblical book.

The Bible contains a variety of literary forms, including short stories, parables, songs, liturgical regulations, letters, epic narratives, and laws. Understanding the literary form of a biblical passage plays an important role in determining the intent of the passage. The Book of Jonah is a case in point. Is the author narrating an actual occurrence of a reluctant prophet's sojourn in the belly of a great fish for three days? Or is the sacred author creating a clever piece of humorous fiction to drive home the point of God's infinite mercy to a hard-hearted Israelite audience? When Jesus tells his disciples it is better to cut off one's hand rather than commit a sin with the hand, he is not advocating self-mutilation. When we understand the Mediterranean use of exaggerated speech to emphasize a point, we understand the teaching behind the exhortation on temptation and are not led astray.

If we pay attention to the forms we find in written literature, we can better understand and correctly interpret what we are reading. In a newspaper, we know an advertisement is trying to sell us something. We know it is going to present only one side of the picture, the most favorable one for its product. We have learned, perhaps through hard experience, that a product may not be as wonderful as the advertisement suggests. In this example of a simple ad, we have applied several rules of interpretation instinctively and perhaps even unconsciously. We should do the same when we attempt to interpret the Bible. But that means we have to learn about the literary forms the biblical writers used and the purpose of these forms. When we understand how they are used within a biblical book, we have a better chance of understanding what the biblical author was trying to say and thereby we can better hear what God is saying to us in our lives.

DOES THE BIBLE CONTAIN ANY MISTAKES?

For many Christians, biblical inspiration is synonymous with inerrancy. In other words, they believe that because the Bible is inspired, it does not contain any errors. In Catholic tradition these two concepts are separate. The teaching on biblical inspiration tells us that the Bible is the Word of God in human words. A separate issue concerns error in the Bible.

Does the Bible contain errors? Yes it does. In the Book of Daniel, the author states that Babylonian King Belshazzar was killed, and "Darius the Mede received the kingdom, being about sixty-two years old" (Daniel 5:30–31). In truth, Darius did not succeed Belshazzar as king. The Persian king, Cyrus the Great, brought an end to the Babylonian kingdom. In Matthew, the evangelist cites Jeremiah as the source for a prophecy about coins used to buy a potters field after the death of Judas. (See Matthew 27:9–10.) However, the prophecy is from Zechariah, not Jeremiah.

In addition, the Old Testament contains a number of glaring contradictions. The most famous example is the number of animals taken on Noah's ark. In one passage, Noah is told to take two of every kind of living thing (Genesis 6:19), but in the next chapter, Noah is told to bring seven pairs of every clean animal and just one pair of every unclean animal (Genesis 7:2). Because of questions like these, the Catholic Church needed to address the whole issue of the reliability of the Scriptures. A number of papal encyclicals attempted to explain these and other difficulties in the Bible, but it was the Second Vatican Council that gave the sharpest summary of the Church's thinking on errors in the Bible. In the Dogmatic Constitution on Divine Revelation the council said:

"...[T]he books of Scripture must be acknowledged as teaching firmly, faithfully, and without error that truth which God wanted put into the sacred writings for the sake of our salvation" (*DV* 11). The operative words here are "that truth which God wanted...for the sake of our salvation." Whether Darius or Cyrus succeeded Belshazzar does not matter; what does matter is the larger truth contained in the story of Daniel and Belshazzar, that is, that God is working behind the scenes for the salvation of those who remain faithful, even when it means standing up against the strongest of earthly powers. The Church's teaching on inerrancy reaffirms the reliability of the Scriptures as a trustworthy guide for our spiritual journey in life; it does not guarantee non-essential details. It becomes even more urgent, then, to understand the intent of a biblical passage in order to appreciate its meaning.

CONCLUSION

Biblical inspiration is a complex teaching of the Catholic Church, and its implications affect how we understand and interpret the sacred Scriptures. Studying the Bible seriously requires a lot of effort. The good news is that Catholic biblical scholars have been doing just that for many centuries, and there are good Catholic biblical commentaries and other resources to help the serious student understand the Scriptures. Understanding the different perceptions of biblical inspiration might make it easier to understand why good Christian people can have such different interpretations of the same biblical passage.

Discussion Questions

1. *What does it mean for you, personally, to say that the Bible is inspired? In what way did the ideas in this chapter influence you?*
2. *Are you surprised that the Bible has errors? Does it affect your belief in the Bible? Why or why not?*
3. *What does the dictation theory of biblical inspiration mean? What is the other common theory about inspiration called? What does it mean?*
4. *How could a human person and God both be the author at the same time? How do you think it happened?*
5. *Why does the Catholic Church propose such a complex theory of inspiration? What is it trying to preserve?*
6. *Why is it important to pay attention to the literary form of a biblical passage?*
7. *Besides the newspaper example in this chapter, what other modern day literary forms can you think of?*

Further Reading

Brown, Raymond E. *Responses to 101 Questions on the Bible.* New York: Paulist Press, 1990.

Collins, Raymond F. "Inspiration." *The New Jerome Biblical Commentary.* Brown, Raymond, Joseph Fitzmyer, and Roland Murphy, eds. (Englewood Cliffs, NJ: Prentice Hall, 1990), 1023–1033.

Farrell, Melvin L. *Getting to Know the Bible: An Introduction to Sacred Scripture for Catholics.* Chicago, IL: ACTA Publications, 2003.

Gaillardetz, Richard R. *By What Authority? A Primer on Scripture, the Magesterium, and the Sense of the Faithful.* Collegeville, MN: Liturgical Press, 2003.

Murdy, Kay. *What Every Catholic Needs to Know About the Bible: A Parish Guide to Bible Study.* San Jose, CA: Resource Publications, 2004.

Ralph, Margaret Nutting. *And God Said What? An Introduction to Biblical Literary Forms.* Revised Edition. New York: Paulist Press, 2003.

CHAPTER 3
Did It Really Happen?
History and the Bible

In our modern world filled with camera phones and security cameras, we rarely ask: "Did it really happen that way?" We are awash in videotape of an event seen from multiple angles. But this visual record is a comparatively new stage in the evolution of our society. When we go back to the time of the Bible, we do not have such undisputable evidence about events. Questions about what really happened are more complicated.

The question posed in the title of this chapter is fundamental to Jews and Christians who look to the Bible as the authority for their faith. The Bible declares that God *acted* in the lives of the Israelites at different times and in most dramatic ways. For Christians, God entered history at a definite point in time and in a certain place as a human being, born of a virgin named Mary. But did these things really happen?

The answers modern scholars are finding have generated enormous debates. As biblical scholars examine these sacred texts, more questions about what really happened arise. Did the events happen the way they are reported in the Bible? Did they happen at all? How a person answers the question will affect the way he or she reads every single page of the Bible.

HOW DID WE GET TO THIS POINT?

For centuries, no one questioned the reliability of the Bible. It was simply accepted as an accurate record of human history, beginning with the creation of the world and culminating in the birth, death, and resurrection of Jesus. But during the Renaissance (fourteenth through sixteenth centuries), the European world began to change in significant ways. A new mind-set formed that looked beyond the established authorities like the Catholic Church for answers grounded in science and reason. Nicolaus Copernicus' discovery that the earth revolved around the sun (1514) was but the first of many investigations that would raise questions about the reliability of the Bible. A century later, Galileo, using a telescope he invented, confirmed Copernicus' theory. He was ordered to recant his findings because they contradicted the Bible. Two centuries later, Charles Darwin's discovery that living organisms evolved along a process of "natural selection" led to bitter debates about science and the Bible which persist even today. The problem, however, is that once a question has been asked, it cannot be "un-asked;" answers must be found. After the seventeenth century, the authority of the Bible was no longer sufficient to resolve the questions.

In the eighteenth and nineteenth centuries, travel to the Holy Land increased as museum curators sought ancient artifacts from newly discovered tombs of the Pharaohs and "digs" throughout the Middle East. Archaeologists became quite adept at identifying the material remains found at different levels of a "tell," the name given to the mounds formed by successive occupants in a particular location over centuries. Archeological sites, however, are mute witnesses to an ancient time. They can tell us that people lived at a site but cannot tell us who those people were, what they did each day, or what they believed. Historians who search for answers to these questions need written records to help fill in the picture. Because there were so few written records from this ancient time in history, historians naturally turned to the Bible as a written source to corroborate what archaeologists had found.

But that would change quickly during this period of exploration. New "documents" carved in fire hardened clay tablets and inscribed on stone walls of newly uncovered structures provided historians with a gold mine of new data about the ancient Near East.

THE QUESTION REMAINS

With the assistance of new translations of ancient documents and the material remains uncovered by archeologists, it would seem that questions about events recorded in the Bible could be laid to rest. Actually, the opposite is true. More questions than ever emerge as the Biblical record collides with archeological and documentary evidence from the ancient Near East.

On one side of the dispute are scholars who use the new finds to prove that the biblical record is unreliable. They argue that historical material found in the Pentateuch (Genesis, Exodus, Leviticus, Numbers, and Deuteronomy) and in the Former Prophets (Joshua, Judges, 1 & 2 Samuel, and 1 & 2 Kings) was invented by a Jewish priestly group during the Persian period (538–333 BCE). These scholars are called minimalists.

On the other side of the debate are conservative and evangelical scholars who are sometimes called maximalists. They contend that archaeological discoveries confirm much of what is recorded in the Bible and propose that if the Bible is reliable in these instances, it should be given the benefit of the doubt in those areas that are unconfirmed either by archaeology or ancient Near Eastern texts. In cases where archaeology would not be expected to find material remains of a people, such as the time of the semi-nomadic patriarchs, maximalist scholars will use circumstantial evidence from the archeological and written records of other cultures that existed at the same time as the patriarchs. It doesn't prove that the patriarchs existed as they are described in the book of Genesis, but it does show that many of the customs mentioned in Genesis were also found in other neighboring cultures.

AN EXAMPLE

One area where biblical minimalists and maximalists collide involves the Exodus from Egypt. The event is central to Israel's identity, and yet there is no archaeological or non-biblical literary evidence that it happened as described in the Bible. Given the lack of any outside evidence of such an event, minimalist scholars have dismissed the biblical story because the events do not map well with what is known about the Egyptian culture. To them, the picture of a pharaoh involved in duplicating plagues upon his own people is ludicrous. For a pharaoh to permit his magicians to turn the Nile into blood, destroying the fish and polluting the canals that irrigated Egypt's cash crop, is inconceivable. The loss of six hundred thousand slaves (Exodus 12:37) would have affected Egypt's economy in a noticeable way, but there are no indications in written records or archaeological data from that time. The logistics of moving approximately two million people out of Egypt and throughout the Sinai Peninsula for forty years is staggering.

Even the date of the Exodus is disputed. Scholarship, in general, places the event during the reign of Rameses II (1290–1224 BCE), even though the Book of Exodus never mentions the pharaoh's name. Archaeological evidence shows that the cities of Pithom and Rameses (Exodus 1:11) were built during this time. But 1 Kings 6:1 marks the date when construction on the Temple in Jerusalem began; it says work started "in the four hundred eightieth year after the Israelites came out of the land of Egypt, in the fourth year of Solomon's reign." If Solomon became king in 962 BCE as is generally accepted, then the Exodus event took place in 1438 BCE. But at that time, the cities of Pithom and Rameses did not exist. Minimalists and other biblical scholars use these points to show that the biblical narrative was never intended to be a historical record of what happened, but rather a song of praise at how Israel's God brought down the most powerful empire in the ancient world. Israelite audiences would have laughed at the foolishness of the pharaoh to challenge Yahweh at every decisive turn in the story.

Maximalists, however, point to an important piece of Egyptian documentation that may support the Exodus story. Toward the end of the thirteenth century, Pharaoh Merneptah (1224–1211 BCE) led his army into Canaan to subdue a number of rebellions. He left a "victory" monument commemorating his battles and the peoples he conquered. The name "Israel" appears in that list, making it the earliest historical record outside of the Bible indicating that a people by that name existed in the land of Canaan. It does not tell us whether this people recently arrived in Canaan or had been there a long time.

WHAT KIND OF HISTORY DO WE FIND IN THE BIBLE?

As archaeology grows more sophisticated and incorporates new methods from the fields of botany, zoology, and climatology and uses new technologies such as GPS (global positioning system) mapping, we can expect to learn even more from an archaeological "dig." We should also expect that in some cases it may confirm the biblical narrative but, in other cases, will raise new questions. How then can the ordinary reader know if the biblical text is true? The question betrays a common presupposition that history can tell us exactly what happened and is therefore true. But professional historians are the first to point out that history is an interpretation and reconstruction of events based on the data at hand; the historian analyzes that data and constructs a plausible picture of what happened. The historian then lets other professionals critique his or her construction. That is the way history is done today, but is that what the biblical authors were trying to do? Perhaps we need to look at our expectations about history.

Walter Brueggemann's insightful article on history and the Old Testament (listed at the end of the chapter) makes several important distinctions when talking about history. He suggests three ways to understand history. First there is the actual event as it happened; he calls this "actual history." Verifying what actually happened in biblical narratives is almost impossible, because the ancients did not have all the technologies that modern society has to preserve the actual event.

Another kind of history Brueggemann calls "remembered" history. It is an account of the past that has been shaped and filtered by the memory of those who have passed it on to later audiences. The purpose of remembered history is not to archive the past, but to reveal the meaning behind some event. I remember when I was a child, my grandfather would tell stories about his rather unconventional life during the "roaring twenties" and the Great Depression. My brothers and I would sit on the floor with wide eyes, listening to every word. Every so often my grandmother would interrupt him, saying, "Dad, you know it didn't happen that way," to which he would reply, "Be quiet, Mother, I'm telling the story, not you!" Was it actual history? Probably not; but it wasn't completely fabricated either. It told us far more about who our grandfather was than the photo scrapbook our grandmother had carefully preserved.

Still another history Brueggemann calls "confessed history." This kind of history is a collection of stories told by believers about how God worked in their lives. The stories "confessed," that is, proclaimed the mighty deeds of God, which led to loud praise or even silent wonder on the part of those who heard this testimony. It was the collective memory of many generations, told and retold in a worship setting, that evoked some kind of response from those who listened. They were not just stories of yesteryear told to satisfy the curiosity of antiquarians. These stories were told to empower the hope of those who waited for God to work with such power again in their lives. I would suggest that it is this kind of "history" that we find in the Bible.

CONCLUSION

In the end, the question "Did it really happen?" is the wrong question to ask. The more important question is what is the purpose of God's Word in this sacred book? The Bible is God's revelation of who God is. God's Word began creation and continued throughout the centuries until it became flesh in Jesus. God spoke this Word, not to set the record straight, but to issue a call to repentance and new life to all who will believe in the one who has made such an audacious promise.

DISCUSSION QUESTIONS

1. *Western civilization changed dramatically during the period known as "The Enlightenment"; some say it changed again with the invention of the modern computer. Would you agree? How have these changes affected the way people look at the world?*

2. *What is a minimalist? How do you think a minimalist would regard the biblical text?*

3. *What is a maximalist? How do you think a maximalist would regard the biblical text?*

4. *What is the difference between Brueggemann's "remembered history" and his "confessed history"?*

5. *What do you think is the purpose of the Bible? How does your answer affect the way you read it?*

FURTHER READING

Brueggemann, Walter. "History." *Reverberations of Faith: A Theological Handbook of Old Testament Themes.* (Louisville, KY: Westminster John Knox Press, 2002), 95–98.

Dever, William G. *What Did the Biblical Writers Know & When Did They Know It?: What Archaeology Can Tell Us About the Reality of Ancient Israel.* Grand Rapids, MI: Wm. B. Eerdmans Publishing Co., 2002.

Hayes, John H. and J. Maxwell Miller. *Israelite and Judean History.* Philadelphia, PA: Trinity Press International, 1990.

Organ, Barbara E. *Is the Bible Fact or Fiction? An Introduction to Biblical Historiography.* New York: Paulist Press, 2004.

Sheler, Jeffery L. *Is the Bible True? How Modern Debates and Discoveries Affirm the Essence of the Scriptures.* San Francisco, CA: HarperSanFrancisco, 1999.

CHAPTER 4
Choosing a Bible Translation: Which One is Right For You?

D an was clearly frustrated when he spoke to me after Mass. He had gone to a popular Christian bookstore to buy a Bible for his daughter, who was going to college. "There were rows and rows of Bibles," he told me. "There were men's Bibles, women's Bibles, teen Bibles in every size and color. Why are there so many? Where did they all come from?" he asked.

Dan's exasperation reminded me how times have changed. When I was a child, there was only one Catholic Bible and it held all the important family records. Today many translations are available, and choosing the translation that best fits your needs can seem complicated.

THE BIRTH OF THE BIBLE AND THE FIRST TRANSLATIONS

Scholars believe that the Law and the Prophets were the first two sections of the Bible to be written by the Israelites while they were in exile in Babylon sometime after 587 BC. In the next couple of centuries before the birth of Christ, the rest of the Hebrew Old Testament was written. The first New Testament writings were Saint Paul's letters, which were written in the mid 1250s. The Gospels were written twenty to thirty years later. Unfortunately, the original manuscripts no longer exist; the leather hides and papyrus materials that contained these sacred words were lost or destroyed. However, copies of the originals were made, and thus began the tradition of preserving the Bible in written form.

The original manuscripts were written in three languages: Hebrew and Aramaic for the Old Testament and Greek for the New. After the conquests of Alexander the Great (333 BCE), most of the ancient world spoke Greek. In time, Jews living outside of Palestine could no longer read Hebrew, so the Old Testament was translated into Greek. This version was called the *Septuagint*, which means "seventy." A legend surrounding this translation tells how seventy translators took that same number of days to translate the Hebrew text into Greek. It remained the most widely read translation among the Christians for centuries.

In the fourth century CE, Saint Jerome translated the Bible into Latin, since Latin had replaced Greek as the common language in the Western half of the Roman Empire. This translation was called the *Vulgate*. It was a stunning achievement that endured the centuries. Only in modern times, and at the insistence of Pope John Paul II, has the Church produced an updated version of the *Vulgate* which is called the *Nova Vulgata*.

Of course Latin and Greek were not the only two languages into which the Bible was translated. In the early Church, the Bible continued to be translated into other languages: Aramaic, Syriac, Coptic and Ethiopic, to name a few. In the Middle Ages, the Church became concerned about erroneous interpretations and restricted all translations except the *Vulgate*.

THE BIBLE IN ENGLISH

In the centuries before the Reformation, a couple of attempts to translate the Bible into English ended in disaster for the translators. John Wycliffe made a translation in the late 1300s, but the translation was condemned and all copies of it were burned. In 1525, William Tyndale attempted another English translation, but it was also condemned, and Tyndale was executed as a heretic.

In the early 1600s, a group of Oxford scholars, exiled from England after the schism wrought by King Henry VIII, began a translation from the *Vulgate* while living in France. This translation was approved by the Church and is known by the name of the two cities in France where the translation was produced: Douay (the Old Testament) and Rheims (the New Testament). The translation was revised by Bishop Richard Challoner in London just before the Revolutionary War broke out in the colonies. This version, the *Douay-Rheims-Challoner Bible*, was the only acceptable English translation in the Catholic Church until modern times.

By the nineteenth century, archaeologists and biblical scholars began discovering ancient documents and artifacts buried in the Middle East. These discoveries helped them decipher other ancient languages, which in turn helped these biblical specialists learn more about the Hebrew, Aramaic, and Greek language of the original manuscripts. Because of these discoveries biblical specialists were able to understand the meaning of Hebrew words that could only be guessed at in earlier translation efforts. New dictionaries in Hebrew and Aramaic were prepared. The time was right for new and better translations of the original texts.

In 1943 Pope Pius XII wrote an encyclical entitled *Divino Afflante Spiritu*. In it, he encouraged Catholic biblical scholars to use all the best methods and scholarship to produce new translations of the Bible from the best Hebrew, Aramaic, and Greek texts available. The Second Vatican Council, in the Dogmatic Constitution on Divine Revelation (*Dei verbum*), continued this direction and encouraged all Catholics to study the Bible. The council also encouraged scholars, working in the original languages of the Bible, to produce new translations for Catholics to read in their own native languages.

DIFFERENT TRANSLATION PHILOSOPHIES

When translating the written word from one language into another, the translator faces a daunting challenge. He or she must first decide which of the thousands of manuscripts in Hebrew, Greek, and Aramaic is the most accurate. Such a step might seem strange to us; we might think the original texts would all be the same. But over the centuries, as manuscripts were copied and recopied, mistakes entered the text. For example, words and phrases were accidentally omitted or copied twice. In an effort to correct the mistake, a copyist often made the situation worse. Thus determining the "best" text is the very foundation for a good translation; however, scholars do not always agree among themselves which is the best manuscript to use. As a result, different translations may be based on different textual traditions. In general, the ordinary reader will not know what actual manuscripts were used, unless he or she pays attention to the text notes in a translation.

Besides determining the best text to translate, the specialist must then decide what words best capture the original text's meaning. Again, scholars will legitimately disagree about the choice of one word over another. The problem is compounded when dealing with ancient biblical language. The meanings of many Hebrew, Aramaic and Greek words are still uncertain. Future discoveries may help unlock these mysteries.

A good translation, however, must be both accurate and readable. While both characteristics are present in most English translations of the Bible today, a translation will still favor one characteristic over the other. These two characteristics reflect two different philosophies of interpretation.

One approach translates the text word for word; it tries to stay close to the original language both in grammar and vocabulary. The *New American Bible* is an example of this kind of translation. A word-for-word translation cannot be slavishly "literal," but it should reflect the meaning of the text as it was written. For example, the Greek text of Mark 6:7 reads (literally): "And he called the twelve and he began them to send out two by two and he gave to them power over the spirits of uncleanness." The translation is accurate, but it is not very readable. The translation in the *New American Bible* reads: "He summoned the Twelve and began to send them out two by two and gave them authority over unclean spirits." The translation is close to the literal text, and it is also readable. That is what a word-for-word translation should do.

Another translation technique is the meaning-for-meaning or dynamic approach. Instead of translating each word of the text literally, the translators attempt to create in the reader the same impact that the original language had on its readers. A dynamic translation of Mark 6:7, as found in the *Good News Bible*, reads: "He called the twelve disciples together and sent them out two by two. He gave them authority over the evil spirits." Notice that the *Good News Bible* translation does not presume that modern readers know what "the Twelve" means. So this dynamic translation adds the word "disciples," which is not in the Greek text but which makes the meaning clearer to modern readers. Similarly, the Greek text literally says "spirits of uncleanness." The translators knew that this phrase means "evil spirits" so they attempt to make the text more readable by translating the meaning, not just the words.

WHAT TRANSLATION TO CHOOSE

Which approach is better? It depends. If you want to read the Bible as a source of inspiration and prayer, then a meaning-for-meaning translation is a better choice. Such translations will be easier to read and understand. The language will be less "Bible English" and will sound more familiar.

However, if you intend to study the Bible, you will want to have a translation that matches the original language of the Bible more closely; in other words, you will want a word-for-word translation. When you are studying a particular passage in a commentary, following the discussion in the commentary is easier if your Bible text is a literal translation of the original language (Hebrew, Aramaic, or Greek).

Armed with the information in this chapter, you may be in a better position to choose the right Bible translation for you. If you are looking for a literal, word-for-word translation, there are three good translations you might want to consider. The *Revised New American Bible,* commissioned by the bishops of the United States, is the translation used at Mass. This is a reliable word-for-word translation prepared by Catholic biblical scholars for Catholic readers in the United States. Recently the New Testament and the Psalms have been revised to make them more readable. A revision of the Old Testament is awaiting final approval.

Another good literal translation is the New Revised Standard Version. Though this translation was prepared by an ecumenical team of biblical scholars, it has received an imprimatur. It cannot be used in the liturgy, but it can be used for Bible study.

If you want a meaning-for-meaning translation, I'd recommend the *New Jerusalem Bible*. Until recently, it was one of the translations of the Bible that could be read at Mass. And it is a good study tool as well. The hardbound copy of this translation has a wealth of footnotes to help explain confusing passages. Another very readable translation is *Today's English Version*, which was sponsored by the American Bible Society. This society publishes many different Bibles using this translation, including The *Good News Bible*, which has an imprimatur. This insures that critical passages on which Catholics and Protestants may disagree will have reliable notes explaining the differences.

CONCLUSION

The Catholic Bible is no longer simply a repository for family records (births, marriages, deaths, and so forth). Pope Pius XII made it possible for Catholics to have many good translations of the Bible. The Second Vatican Council encouraged Catholics to study the entire Bible and to allow God's Word to challenge their particular outlook and day-to-day behavior. Now it is up to us.

DISCUSSION QUESTIONS

1. *Why are there so many translations of the Bible available today? Do we really need all these different translations?*
2. *What is the difference between a word-for-word translation and a meaning-for-meaning translation?*
3. *Do you have a favorite Bible you read all the time? What translation is it? Why do you like it?*
4. *Do you have more than one Bible in your house? Why do you think it would be helpful to have several different translations of the Bible?*
5. *If you have access to more than one translation of the Bible, look up Exodus 6:12. What excuse does Moses give for not wanting to speak God's Word to the pharaoh? (Hint: the Hebrew text says, "I have uncircumcised lips.")*
6. *Why was the Old Testament translated into Greek? Why was the Bible then translated into Latin, Coptic, Syriac, and several other ancient languages?*
7. *The process of determining which of the oldest biblical manuscripts still in existence today is closest to the original text of the Bible is called "textual criticism." Why is such a process necessary?*

FURTHER READING

Kubo, Sakae and Walter Specht. *So Many Versions? Twentieth Century English Versions of the Bible.* Revised edition. Grand Rapids, MI: Zondervan, 1983.

Pilch, John J. *Choosing a Bible Translation.* Collegeville, MN: Liturgical Press, 2000.

Sheely, Steven M. and Robert N. Nash, Jr. *The Bible in English Translation: An Essential Guide.* Nashville, TN: Abingdon Press, 1997.

CHAPTER 5
Bible Study:
A Catholic Approach

"Why is Bible study so hard?" is a question I am repeatedly asked when conducting parish Bible study programs. I often tell people that when I was young, I said the same thing about learning to ride a bike. Bible study is a skill anyone can learn, even if there seem to be more obstacles than avenues.

Bible study does take work. You wouldn't think that God's Word would be difficult to understand, but we must remember that God inspired human authors more than two thousand years ago. Obviously, these authors did not speak English and lived in cultures very different from ours. The Hebrew, Aramaic, and Greek languages presuppose a whole different way of thinking, but differences in language is only one of the hurdles we face in trying to understand the Bible. Differences in culture, values, and societal roles pose an even greater challenge for the modern-day Bible student.

If you want to study the Bible, I believe you need four things: resources, a method of study, a block of time that you can devote to your study without a lot of interruptions, and a resolution to stop putting it off and to start today.

GATHERING BIBLE STUDY RESOURCES

Many people have a favorite Bible that they've had a long time; it may even be an heirloom. Use that favorite Bible for your own spiritual reading and growth, but plan to get a "working" Bible, that is, one that you will write in and mark up. With recent archaeological discoveries, scholars today understand the original Scripture texts better. Getting a new translation will enable you to take advantage of these discoveries and notes that go with the translation. I suggest that you obtain two or three modern translations of the Bible. The translations I recommend are the *Revised New American Bible*, the *New Jerusalem Bible*, the New Revised Standard Version (a Catholic edition), and *Today's English Version* (a Catholic edition).

Another resource you will want to have on hand is a Bible atlas. Many Bibles contain maps, and these are fine to use. But a Bible atlas will have many more maps with greater detail, as well as several cross-referencing indices so that you can find strange sounding biblical cities and locales. Besides an atlas, you should obtain a good Bible dictionary such as *Eerdmans Dictionary of the Bible*. While it may be expensive (about $45), perhaps you could suggest it as a birthday or anniversary gift.

Finally you should get a good introductory book on the Old Testament and another one for the New Testament. Some recommendations are included at the end of this chapter. It is important to read an introduction to the Old Testament and a separate one for the New. Christians naturally read the Old Testament in light of their understanding of the New Testament, and as a result, they often limit themselves to the passages in the Old Testament that point to the life and ministry of Jesus. But that approach can also blind the Christian reader to the message of the Old Testament itself. Reading separate introductory works can help you pay attention to the Old Testament environment and the world of the New Testament without mixing the two. A good introduction will also have an introduction to each book of the Bible, which will help you understand the background and culture of the human author of that book.

IT'S ALL IN THE METHOD

While gathering a small collection of resources is a preliminary step to serious Bible study, you will also need a practical method you can put into use. The first step in this method of Bible study is to say a prayer to the Holy Spirit. Although it is the simplest step, it is without doubt the most important. Studying the Bible is not just an academic exercise. God is speaking to us in this holy Word. We will need to do many things to ensure that we are listening to God's Word in the best way possible, but asking the Holy Spirit to help us hear this Word will prepare the way for everything else.

After that, the method I propose involves three steps: read, compare and research. It will help to have a notebook handy so that you can write down thoughts and questions that come to you while employing this method. For the sake of example, I've chosen a short text from Paul's first letter to the Thessalonians (4:3–8). First, read the passage in a modern Bible translation; then read it again. If it won't disturb anyone, read it again, this time out loud to an imaginary group of people who do not have the text in front of them. Then write a short summary of the text in your own words. For this particular passage, I wrote: "Paul tells the Thessalonians that God is calling them to holiness. How? Paul suggests three ways: (1) avoid sexual immorality, (2) develop good marriage relationships, and (3) treat everyone in the community with fairness. This call from God is not optional, but God gives the grace to carry it out through the Holy Spirit."

Next, take one verse at a time and read the same verse in each of your Bible translations. In this example I use the New Revised Standard Version (NRSV), the *Revised New American Bible* (*RNAB*), and *Today's English Version* (*TEV*) for comparison. The *RNAB* uses the word "holiness," while the NRSV uses "sanctification." These two words may appear to be synonyms, but there is a difference between the two meanings. It shows that the underlying Greek word has a range of meanings. What did Paul mean when he used that word? For now, just make a note of it in your notebook.

In the same verse there is another difference between translations. In the NRSV, Paul warns the community to specifically avoid fornication, but the *RNAB* uses a more general term, "immorality," and the *TEV* describes it as "sexual immorality." The differences here are significant; you might write in your notebook the question: "What kind of immorality is Paul describing in verse 3?"

This kind of comparison requires careful attention and thus can seem very tedious. However, it does force one to examine the text more closely. The purpose of this comparison is to see differences. Some of these differences will be explained in a good commentary—but don't go there just yet.

Something very interesting happens in verse 4 that you wouldn't notice unless comparing translations. Read the verse in each translation, ignoring for the moment any footnotes attached to it. In the *RNAB*, Paul talks about "how to acquire a wife," but in the NRSV, he speaks about "how to control your own body," and the *TEV* speaks of "how to live with your wife." If all three translations are based on the same Greek text, why would the NRSV be so completely different? Is Paul addressing the men in the community and urging them to exercise sexual self-control, or is he warning them about marital infidelity? Now go back and check the footnotes. In effect, the notes say the text is ambiguous; it could mean both things. Once again, make a note in your notebook.

As you work through all the verses, the method is the same: (1) look at the verse in each translation, one at a time, and note the differences that you find; (2) examine any footnotes that are present to see whether they help explain the differences; (3) write any questions and observations from your careful comparison in your notebook.

Researching Your Resources

The final step in your Bible study is to look up background information that could help explain a particular passage. Here is where a good Bible dictionary can be very helpful. A Bible dictionary will explain, for example, the meaning of the word "holiness" in both the Old and New Testaments. In this case, knowing the Old Testament meaning is helpful since Paul was a Pharisee, steeped in the Jewish traditions of the Old Testament.

My Bible dictionary said the Sadducees believed that holiness was found in the Temple and in the sacrifices offered there. The Pharisees believed that holiness was more personal and took root in one's home and family. If Paul was a Pharisee, would that color how he understood holiness? Could that be why Paul is concerned about marriage in this passage on holiness? These questions may not have answers yet, but I would write them down as part of my research.

A Bible dictionary is useful for obtaining background information. Look up the article on 1 Thessalonians. Paul wrote this letter to encourage the fledgling Christian community in Thessalonica and to answer some of its questions. He was concerned about conduct within the Christian community and the way its members related with those who were not part of the community. Paul wanted them to be above blame in all moral matters, since their opponents were looking for any failure to justify more persecution.

If a Bible dictionary is not available, read the introduction to 1 Thessalonians in your Bible. It will generally provide an outline of the book and some background about the author and the audience. The *New Jerusalem Bible* has a very good introduction to each book of the Bible and wonderful footnotes on every page.

If you have a good introduction to the New Testament, such as the one by Pheme Perkins listed at the end of this chapter, it would be helpful to read about Paul's letters. What were letters like in Paul's day? How were they written? Then look at the chapter dealing with the Letters to the Thessalonians. A good introductory book on the New Testament will give you enough information to understand the audience to whom Paul wrote and perhaps a better sense of why Paul wrote this letter in the first place.

Now that you have read the text, compared translations, and conducted some basic research, you should have a number of questions and comments written in your notebook. Read the passage one more time and ask yourself what Paul is saying to the Thessalonians and how you think it applies to you. Write down any questions you would like to ask Paul. At this point, you are ready to turn to a commentary and read what it says about this particular passage.

In the commentary I used, the author noted the difficulty of interpreting verse 4. The commentator noted that even saints in the Church have disagreed about what Paul was saying. Because we compared translations, we can appreciate the problem. Is Paul talking about controlling one's own sexual desires, or is he talking about marriage? One way to understand this passage is to see how Paul becomes more specific in his warnings. First he warns about sexual immorality, in general, then he encourages marriages that are clothed in respect and honor, and finally he warns against adultery, which destroys trust within the growing Christian community. When I first read the passage, I did not realize that Paul was talking about the effect of adultery on the community. I thought he was urging that everyone treat one another with respect. Only after doing this kind of careful study, can I now understand what Paul was trying to say.

UNDERSTANDING THE BIBLE TAKES TIME

Each time you use the method I've described here, your knowledge of the Bible will grow, and your notebooks will continually refresh your memory. A Catholic interpretation of the Bible requires an understanding of the human author's time, background, culture, and religious influences, as well as the audience for whom the author wrote. This knowledge then helps us understand the meaning of the human author, which is essential if we hope to hear what the Divine Author wanted to express.

A willingness to begin is perhaps the most crucial element in Bible study. Start gathering resources today, even if it will take several months or more to get some of the resources mentioned in this chapter. Pick a particular book of the Bible that interests you. Review the steps of this method, and start reading and studying today. If God is speaking to us through the words of holy Scripture—and I firmly believe God is—then we shouldn't want to miss a single word or wait another minute.

DISCUSSION QUESTIONS

1. *Why is Bible study hard for Catholics today?*
2. *Older Bibles may have a personal value, but they are not very useful for doing a Bible study. Give some reasons why they may not be as helpful.*
3. *What is a Bible atlas? Why is it useful for Bible study?*
4. *Have you ever used a biblical commentary? Was it helpful to you? Why or why not?*
5. *What is the purpose of the method presented in this chapter for studying the Bible?*
6. *Why does the author suggest having a notebook handy when studying the Bible?*

FURTHER READING

Bible Dictionaries

Eerdmans Dictionary of the Bible. Beck, Astrid B., David Noel Freedman, and Allen C. Myers, eds. Grand Rapids: Wm. B. Eerdmans Publishing Company, 2000.

The HarperCollins Bible Dictionary. Revised and updated edition. Achtemeier, Paul J., ed. New York: HarperCollins Publishing, 1996.

Bible Atlases

Atlas of the Bible Lands. Frank, Harry Thomas, ed. Maplewood, N.J.: Hammond World Atlas Corp., 2007.

The Collegeville Atlas of the Bible. Harpur, James and Marcus Braybrooke, eds. Collegeville, MN: The Liturgical Press, 1999.

General Introductions to the Old Testament

Anderson, Bernhard W. *Understanding the Old Testament*. Fifth edition. Upper Saddle River, NJ: Pearson Prentice Hall, 2007.

Boadt, Lawrence. *Reading the Old Testament: An Introduction*. New York: Paulist Press, 1984.

Coogan, Michael D. *The Old Testament: A Historical and Literary Introduction to the Hebrew Scriptures*. New York: Oxford University Press, 2005.

General Introductions to the New Testament

Cory, Catherine. *A Voyage Through the New Testament*. Upper Saddle River, NJ: Pearson Prentice Hall, 2007.

Johnson, Luke Timothy. *The Writings of the New Testament: An Interpretation*. Revised edition. Minneapolis, MN: Augsburg Fortress Press, 2004.

Perkins, Pheme. *Reading the New Testament: An Introduction*. Second edition. New York: Paulist Press, 1988.

PART TWO

Reading the Old Testament

CHAPTER 6
How to Read the Pentateuch With Understanding

R eading the Pentateuch shouldn't be that hard, but for many, it is. Genesis, the first book of the Pentateuch, starts off well with a majestic narrative of creation. It gets interesting, both in and outside the Garden of Eden, but then we hit the brakes at a genealogy or two. The stories about the patriarchs and Moses are appealing, but then we come to a halt again at the roadblock of guidelines for a couple of Jewish festivals. Before we can get back up to speed, we skid to a complete stop at a rockslide of laws that came down from a mountain in the Sinai desert. Some people will forge on and read the whole thing, motivated by a sense of duty, but most people are a wreck by the time they reach Leviticus. Should something be this hard to read?

The word *Pentateuch* comes from a Greek word that means "five containers," each of which held a written scroll. It refers to the first five books of the Old Testament: Genesis, Exodus, Leviticus, Numbers, and Deuteronomy. For Jews, these five books form the most sacred part of their Scriptures, the Torah, a Hebrew word that often gets translated as "the Law." However, "law" is not an adequate translation. The problem with reading the Pentateuch stems mostly from our misunderstanding of what we are reading. We approach the five books separately and read them like any other book in the Bible. We tend to think they were simply written to record the history of the Jewish people before the time of Christ. This assumption colors our interest and our expectations.

GETTING OUR BEARINGS

The first thing a reader should know is that the Pentateuch should be read as a whole, as one book. Each of the five books in this rather large work is only a *part* of the story. It is also important to remember that not all of the Pentateuch is meant to be read in the same way. Some parts are a collection of laws; other parts are lists of tribal boundaries, genealogies, and census data. These parts are important, but only if one has a specific interest in these matters; not everyone does. Third we should keep in mind that the story really begins in Genesis 12 when God directly invites an aging nomadic shepherd and his family to move, once again, to a new land. Genesis 1—11 is really a "prequel" to the story that begins in Genesis 12; it tells us why God decided to call this particular tribesman and why Abraham's "yes" to God's plan begins a story worth telling and reading. In the middle of this story, we find Israel encamped in the Sinai desert at the base of a mountain by the same name, while Moses has gone up the mountain to receive God's law for the people. At this point we encounter a large body of laws. Exodus 25—31 and 35—40, the entire book of Leviticus, and Numbers 1—10 are civil and cultic law codes. There is another large body of laws in Deuteronomy 12—26. Unless one has a specific interest in the application of a particular law, this material can be set aside for later reference.

Another important issue when reading these five books is the question of authorship: who wrote the Pentateuch? The traditional answer is seemingly straightforward—Moses; it is one that has been accepted by Jews and Christians for centuries. While it has been the traditional answer, it is not a simple one. How did Moses do that? Where did he get all the information found in the five books of the Pentateuch, when according to the book of

Exodus, Moses only got involved in this story as an adult inspecting a burning bush? Again the simple answer is that God told Moses everything, and he wrote it down. But this simple answer raises more questions: when did Moses write down all of this information? While on Mount Sinai? Or while leading roughly two million people through the Sinai desert for forty years? Then of course there is the matter about Moses' death. There had to be a second "author" involved in the Pentateuch who completed the book of Deuteronomy (34:5–12), since this material tells what happened after Moses died.

Even beyond the logistical problem of how Moses actually wrote the Pentateuch, there are several clues within the Pentateuch that more than one author was involved. One indication of multiple authors is the presence of duplicate stories throughout the Pentateuch. There are two creation stories (Genesis 1:1–2:4 and Genesis 2:5–25). There are two versions of the great flood in Genesis 6—9. Abraham attempts to save himself twice in a foreign land by pretending his wife, Sarah, is really his sister (Genesis 12:10–20; 20:1–18). God makes a covenant twice with Abraham (Genesis 15 and 17). Jacob's name is changed to "Israel" twice (Genesis 32:25–33; 35:9–10). There are two versions of the Ten Commandments (Exodus 20:1–17 and Deuteronomy 5:6–18).

Another clue is the way certain individuals and places have two distinct names. God is called Yahweh sometimes and Elohim at other times. Also Mount Sinai is sometimes called Mount Horeb. Moses' father-in-law is called Jethro sometimes and Reuel at others. There are also a number of contradictions in the stories. Before the flood, God decides to set the limit for human life to one hundred twenty years, but after the flood, Noah lives to be three hundred fifty years old. In the genealogies that follow in Genesis 11:10–23, everyone lives quite a bit longer. When Moses encounters God at the burning bush, God tells him that his name, Yahweh, was unknown to the patriarchs: Abraham, Isaac, and

Jacob (Exodus 6:3); yet each of the patriarchs refers to God using the name "Yahweh."

For all of the above reasons and several more, modern biblical scholars have rejected the notion that Moses was the sole author of the Pentateuch. Literary specialists began to pay attention to the narratives in these five books and noticed several different literary styles. Towards the end of the nineteenth century, a man named Julius Wellhausen proposed a possible solution that accounted for these discrepancies. He suggested that the work of four different authors was combined to form the five scrolls that made up the Pentateuch. His suggestion is known as the Documentary Hypothesis, and for about a century, biblical scholars generally accepted his ideas with some modifications along the way. In the last twenty-five years, the hypothesis has drawn a fair amount of criticism and has been rejected by some scholars. However, even their proposed solutions build upon the basic premise of the Documentary Hypothesis that the Pentateuch is composed of several different points of view, and that the formation of these five books was more complex than previously thought.

In the Documentary Hypothesis, the four authors are each given a single letter for their name that represents some characteristic about them. The authors wrote their work at different times and in different locations, and these differences have affected how they perceived God. The oldest document was written by someone who used the name Yahweh for God. In German, the name Yahweh is spelled *Jahwe*; since German scholarship developed this hypothesis, this author is called "J." Another author, named "E," refers to God as Elohim. Scholars believe that J was the oldest document written in the ninth or tenth century. The E document was put into written form about a hundred years later. Both documents were combined soon after, since they told similar stories, though with very different points of view. Scholars refer to this combined document as JE.

A third author, "D," is the only author associated with a single book in the Pentateuch: Deuteronomy. This author, whose distinct vocabulary and style of writing borders almost on preaching, may have been responsible for the "law code" found in the Temple during the time of King Josiah, which became the basis for a great reform of the people in the sixth century BCE (2 Kings 22—23). The final and most prominent document is called P. The letter stands for the priests who survived the destruction of Jerusalem in 587 BCE and were responsible for keeping the Jewish faith alive while the people lived in exile in Babylon. These priests are credited with the great creation account in Genesis 1 and most of the laws and genealogies that make up the Pentateuch. It was this group, the priests, who incorporated the work of J, E, and D into their narrative and then separated the combined narrative into five scrolls, forming the Pentateuch as we have it today.

Though the Documentary Hypothesis is complex, it draws attention to the reality of this five-volume work: it was not written all at one time by one author. If a person wants to understand the Pentateuch, then he or she must listen to the voice of each of the authors and become attuned to their individual styles of writing.

CONCLUSION

Sometimes when people hear the word "Torah" they think of "laws." The New Testament uses that term often to refer to the Old Testament: "the law of Moses" (Luke 2:22), "the law and the prophets" (Matthew 5:17). But calling it "the Law" carries with it a negative sense of excessive legalism; the picture of the Pharisees and Sadducees, in the New Testament, is one of endless argument over minute details of the law.

But the Torah is more than just a collection of laws about worship and sacrifices in a Temple that does not even exist anymore. It is a collection of family stories about people who struggled to understand what God was doing in their lives. It is the story of a covenant way of life that resulted from an incredible act of liberation. Many of these stories were told and retold when the people gathered to worship God. Israel remembered who it was and who it was called to be in these times of worship. And in time, laws were added to this story to insure the practice of this worship. But it was the story that Israel celebrated, not the laws.

The word *torah* comes from a Hebrew verb which means "to throw." In time it came to designate the instruction of children by their parents. Instruction is a better translation than law. Think about how you might instruct your children about the important things they need to know in life. Is their identity found only in a number of laws to be kept? Don't play in the street. Don't talk to strangers. Don't talk back to your parents. A child's formation is far more than just rules; it is also about family celebrations. It is hearing from grandparents, aunts, and uncles about their parents' lives when they were young. The formation continues when they learn the prayers their parents were taught and embrace the values that their parents live each day.

The early Christian communities returned to the stories in the Torah even as they moved away from its laws and ways of worship. It was both the Torah and the Prophets that helped the early Christian preachers understand what Jesus had done. And though today Christians are more comfortable with the New Testament, they are in danger of losing their roots if they skip over the stories of *their* ancestors in faith, in the Pentateuch, because it is too hard to read.

DISCUSSION QUESTIONS

1. *Have you ever read the entire Pentateuch from beginning to end? If you did, what was your experience like? If you did not, why not?*

2. *Although it was believed for centuries that Moses was the author of the Pentateuch, what are some indications in the text that there may have been more than one author?*

3. *The Torah is also called "the Law of Moses." After reading this chapter, is that title an adequate understanding of the Torah today?*

4. *What is the Documentary Hypothesis, and what was its key insight into the composition of the Pentateuch?*

5. *What does the word "torah" actually mean? How does this meaning help you understand these first five books of the Bible?*

6. *Does the Pentateuch have anything to say to Christians today?*

FURTHER READING

Brueggemann, Walter and Hans Walter Wolff. *The Vitality of Old Testament Traditions.* Second edition. Atlanta, GA: Westminster John Knox Press, 1985.

Campbell, Antony F. and Mark A. O'Brien. *Sources of the Pentateuch: Texts, Introductions, Annotations.* Minneapolis, MN: Fortress Press, 1993.

Friedman, Richard Elliott. *The Bible With Sources Revealed: A New View Into the Five Books of Moses.* New York: HarperOne, 2005.

McDermott, John J. *Reading the Pentateuch: A Historical Introduction.* New York: Paulist Press, 2002.

Murphy, Roland E. *101 Questions & Answers on the Biblical Torah: Reflections on the Pentateuch.* New York: Paulist Press, 2003.

Ska, Jean-Louis. *Introduction to Reading the Pentateuch.* Sr. Pascale Dominique, trans. Winona Lake, IN: Eisenbrauns, 2006.

CHAPTER 7
The Deuteronomic History: Is It Real or Religious?

The Pentateuch comes to a conclusion with the people of God gathered outside the Promised Land in an area that, today, is part of the land of Jordan. Looking across the Jordan River, they could see the land. However, before they entered, Moses wanted to give them one last "sermon." That sermon is called the book of Deuteronomy. In this "sermon," Moses makes clear that God placed two gifts before the people: the land *and* the covenant. The two realities are deeply interconnected; Israel cannot have one without the other. The history that unfolded after the people entered the Promised Land, however, revealed that Israel only saw the one gift and sadly lost even that. This history begins with the Book of Joshua and ends with the second Book of Kings. Biblical scholars call it the Deuteronomic History (Dhistory).

WHAT IS THE DEUTERONOMIC HISTORY (DHISTORY)?

The DHistory is a term that modern biblical scholars give to six books in the Old Testament that deal with Israel's history from the time it entered the Promised Land under the leadership of Joshua until the moment it lost possession of this land to a Babylonian king, Nebuchadnezzar, in 587/86 BCE. These six books are: Joshua, Judges, 1 & 2 Samuel, and 1 & 2 Kings. They cover approximately six hundred years of Israel's history (1220–586 BCE).

In the Jewish Bible, these books are considered part of the Prophets. The Jewish canon is divided into three parts: the Law, the Prophets, and the Writings. The Prophetic books are subdivided into two parts: The Former Prophets and the Latter Prophets. This history of Israel is part of the Former Prophets. It might seem strange to us that these apparently historical books were considered part of Israel's prophetic heritage; that placement should remind us the Jews themselves did not regard these books as an objective, dispassionate presentation of historical fact. *Confessed History*

The more traditional Christian view treats these six books as separate works with separate authors. The Book of Joshua was thought to be written by Joshua himself; the Book of Judges was written by an unknown author who lived during the early days of Samuel. The Books of Samuel were written by the prophets Samuel, Nathan, and Gad. The author of the Book of Kings is unknown. The problem with the separate authorship of these books is that it overlooks the theological themes that run through these books as a whole.

In 1943, a biblical scholar, Martin Noth, suggested that these six books were originally a unified work produced by the same author or authors who wrote the book of Deuteronomy. That is why scholars today refer to this collection as the Deuteronomic History or DHistory. The book of Deuteronomy acted as a "hinge" book. It concludes the Pentateuch with the death of Moses and sets a number of themes that will resurface in the DHistory. What Noth found particularly interesting was the way the theology expressed in Deuteronomy was used to evaluate the unfolding events described in the DHistory.

The DHistory is, first, a history. It uses historical sources and data from royal archives; it even identifies them by name: the Book of Jashar (Joshua 10:13), the Book of the Acts of Solomon (1 Kings 11:41), the Annals of the Kings of Judah (1 Kings 14:29), and the Annals of the Kings of Israel (1 Kings 14:19). Unfortunately these sources no longer exist, so we cannot compare them with the DHistory. The author(s) also used pre-existing narratives and inserted them into the history. The most important of these independent narratives is called "the Succession Narrative" (2 Samuel 9—24; 1 Kings 1—2). Like a short novel with a large cast of characters, it tells the story of how Solomon became king after David against all odds. But the DHistory is more than just a historical reference work; it is a religious history. The author(s) selected certain pieces from the material available and reshaped it along the lines of a few controlling religious themes.

POSSIBLE THEMES WITHIN THE DHISTORY

That Jews consider these books to be part of the prophetic canon of their Bible draws attention to the fact that prophets play a large role in these books. Samuel, Elijah and Elisha are prophets who were major characters in Israel's history. Many other lesser known prophets appear briefly in the pages of these books: Gad (1 Samuel 22:5), Nathan (2 Samuel 7:2), Ahijah the Shilonite (1 Kings 11:29), Jehu (1 Kings 16:7), Micaiah (1 Kings 22:8), and references to several unnamed prophets throughout 1 & 2 Kings.

The DHistory also illustrates the way the prophetic word was *fulfilled* in Israel's history. In 1 Kings 11:26–40, the prophet Ahijah told Jeroboam, a servant of King Solomon, that God was going to divide Solomon's kingdom as a punishment for the growing idolatry in the kingdom; the prophecy was fulfilled very soon thereafter in 1 Kings 12:15–16. Again in 1 Kings 13:2, an unnamed prophet received God's word that a child in the line of David would, one day, end the corrupt religious practices in the southern kingdom; his name would be Josiah. Indeed, a Davidic king named Josiah, born almost three hundred years later, brought about a monumental reform of Israel's worship (2 Kings 23:16–18). Given this interest in prophets and their prophecies, it is understandable that Jewish scriptures included these books in their prophetic canon.

Another theme running through the DHistory is the demand for true worship of God without combining elements from the Canaanite worship practices. For some scholars, this is the main theme of the work. In the books of Samuel and Kings, we find an evaluation of all the kings, both in the northern kingdom of Israel and the southern kingdom of Judah. It is not based on what they built or the wars they won, but rather how well they preserved the true worship of God. On this criterion alone they were judged a failure. Time and again the reader encounters a similar summary: "He did what was evil in the sight of the Lord, walking in the way of his ancestor and in the sin that he (Jeroboam) caused Israel to commit" (1 Kings 15:26). The names of the kings change throughout the narrative, but the summary assessment remains the same.

In 1 Kings 18, the two themes of prophet and the proper worship of Yahweh come together in a dramatic contest between the prophet Elijah and four hundred fifty prophets of the Canaanite god, Baal. The dramatic confrontation takes place on Mount Carmel when Elijah challenges the Canaanite prophets to ask their god to consume, by fire, their sacrifice, while he does the same with Yahweh. The contest is intended to convince Israelites who are still "on the fence" about the need to worship Yahweh alone (1 Kings 18:21). In an unmistakable display of power, God consumes Elijah's sacrifice, while the prophets of Baal get no response and are slain for their failure to produce results.

This key narrative in the DHistory highlights the central challenge that Israel faced throughout its history. It lived in a land that accepted the worship of an alien god, Baal, and time and again, Israel was tempted to participate in this idolatry. The religion of Baal fostered an expectation that the Canaanite gods could be manipulated to meet one's own *personal* needs: make my flocks fertile, give me a bountiful harvest. It led to a distorted understanding of the relationship between God and humans where self-interest was the primary motive for worship. (For Israel, the worship of Yahweh went hand-in-hand with a call to care for the orphan, the widow, and the stranger.) Though Elijah won his battle against Baal, the northern kingdom of Israel did not. The fall of this kingdom in 722 BCE to Assyria was in fact God's judgment on their religious waffling.

One final theme that appears in this religious history is the necessity of obedience to God's covenant. Keeping the covenant that God made with Israel was another criterion in the evaluation of Israel's kings. Because the Israelites refused to commit themselves wholeheartedly to Yahweh, the northern kingdom fell to Assyria (2 Kings 17:13–14). A little more than a century later, the same fate would befall the southern kingdom and its capital city of Jerusalem. King David, on his deathbed, had warned Solomon that if he kept the covenant faithfully he would not fail (1 Kings 2:1–4), but sadly, Solomon and most of the kings of Judah after him failed to heed this prophetic warning.

WHO WROTE THE DHISTORY?

Deuteronomy was thought to be written by D, a letter that scholars gave to an author or authors who wrote this book during the time of Jeremiah the prophet. Large sections of Jeremiah have the same exhortative style and vocabulary as found in Deuteronomy. Because of the many references to prophets in the DHistory and the pattern of "prediction-fulfillment" running throughout it, some biblical scholars believe a group of prophets who lived in the northern kingdom of Israel were responsible for the basic text of the DHistory. Another group, priests who belonged to the tribe of Levi, the same tribe from which Moses descended, was responsible for much of the book of Deuteronomy. The location of both of these groups is important for our understanding of their works. After Solomon died, the kingdom established by David split into two. One kingdom called Israel encompassed most of the northern territory of Palestine, which once belonged to ten of the tribes of Jacob. The other smaller kingdom, Judah, included Jerusalem and some land to the south. The two kingdoms were quite different. In the northern kingdom, the life and teachings of Moses were preserved, while in the south, the accomplishments of David were celebrated. The first king of the northern kingdom of Israel, Jeroboam, decided to build two sanctuaries in his kingdom to make it easier for people to worship God and to replace the pilgrimages to the Temple in Jerusalem. The decision had disastrous consequences for his kingdom. If the kingdom could have two sanctuaries, why couldn't there be more? His decision facilitated the eventual acceptance of other gods, goddesses, and worship centers throughout the northern kingdom.

A prophetic group in the northern kingdom saw the increase in worship of the foreign gods and brought God's Word to the kings and people alike, but their message fell on deaf ears. These prophets could see a pattern repeating itself: the king and people would disregard their covenant obligations, which provoked God's punishment. The people would repent, and God would forgive their violations. Then the cycle would begin again. With each cycle, both king and people grew more insensitive to what they were doing. When the northern kingdom of Israel fell to Assyria in 721 BCE, members of this prophetic group and the Levitical priests knew exactly why it had happened. Many of them fled south into the kingdom of Judah for refuge, and they saw the same disregard of God's covenant in the southern kingdom. They also saw the unbelievable arrogance of the Davidic monarchy, which believed God had promised David's dynasty would never end, so they were divinely protected from what had happened in the northern kingdom. This Deuteronomic group knew that the destruction of the southern kingdom of Judah was inevitable. When it happened, they wrote a history beginning with Joshua's faithful leadership as the successor of Moses and concluding with the destruction of Jerusalem in 587 BCE to Nebuchadnezzar's Babylonian army. This showed that what happened was not some terrible unexpected calamity, but simply the culmination, over six centuries, of continual covenant neglect.

CONCLUSION

These six books tell the story of Israel's brief rise to power on the world stage and its long slow demise to more powerful neighbors. It is a national history that incorporates extraordinary figures like Moses, Joshua, Samuel, David, and Solomon and an almost systemic blindness to what it meant to be God's Chosen People. The DHistory was ultimately read by Jews in Babylonian captivity after the destruction of Jerusalem. Once again, the Chosen People found themselves outside of "their" land, a land now inhabited by foreigners. As they listened to Moses' exhortations to their ancestors long ago, they must have said to themselves: *If only we had listened and remembered!* The enduring gift of the DHistory for those Jews in Babylonian exile was a chance to clearly see what went wrong and why, as they waited to begin again.

DISCUSSION QUESTIONS

1. *What is the Deuteronomic History? Why do biblical scholars use that term?*
2. *Why does the Jewish Bible include these books among their prophetic books and call them the "Former Prophets?"*
3. *Is the DHistory a historical work or a theological narrative? Why?*
4. *What are some of the distinctive themes that run throughout the DHistory?*
5. *Who were the Levites? What is their contribution to the DHistory?*
6. *Why does this religious history insist on the worship of Yahweh alone and obedience to the covenant?*

FURTHER READING

Campbell, Antony F. and Mark A. O'Brien. *Unfolding the Deuteronomistic History: Origins, Upgrades, Present Text*. Minneapolis, MN: Fortress Press, 2000.

Doorly, William J. *Obsession with Justice: The Story of the Deuteronomists*. New York: Paulist Press, 1994.

McKenzie, Steven L. *Covenant*. St. Louis, MO: Chalice Press, 2000.

Nelson, Richard D. *The Historical Books*. Nashville, TN: Abingdon Press, 1998.

Organ, Barbara E. *Is the Bible Fact or Fiction? An Introduction to Biblical Historiography*. New York: Paulist Press, 2004.

CHAPTER 8
The Power of the Prophetic Word

When we hear the word *prophet,* several images may come to mind. We might think of a person who can see into the future and thus make predictions about what is to happen. Warren Buffet, a very wealthy investor, is known as the "oracle of Omaha" because of his successful investment decisions. But we might also think of a prophet as someone with great religious sensitivity. Such a person sees reality at a much deeper level than the ordinary person does. The words of Mother Teresa of Calcutta or the writings of Pope John Paul II are thought to be prophetic. Still we might think of a social activist who courageously speaks out against injustice in our world such as the late Martin Luther King, Jr., or Archbishop Desmond Tutu; they are often referred to as modern day prophets. All of these activities have been labeled "prophetic" at one time or another, and they may color our understanding of the prophets in the Bible.

The English word *prophet* comes from the Greek word *prophētēs* which literally means "to speak on behalf of another." The Greek word, however, is a translation of one of the Hebrew words for a prophet: *nabî'*. While experts still argue over the meaning of that word, most scholars believe it means "one who is chosen or called." From the definitions of both the Greek and the Hebrew words, we could say that a biblical prophet was both a messenger sent to speak a message from God and someone who was painfully aware of the demands of this vocation.

The Old Testament is full of prophets. Some are famous, such as Isaiah, Jeremiah, and Elijah. Others are not as well known, such as Nathan (see 2 Samuel 7:2). Some are complete strangers, such as Uriah (see Jeremiah 26:20–23). These prophets did not all function in the same way. In ancient times, some prophets were associated with a temple and participated in religious functions. People could ask a cultic prophet in the temple to seek an oracle from a particular god in answer to their request. Like pilgrims at sacred shrines today, ancient souls needed a word of reassurance or direction in times of crisis. Prophets located at the royal court of the king may have been expected to bring a positive message to the king about a future event or war that would be resolved in the king's favor. And bands of roving prophets would go throughout the countryside, falling into rhythmic trances and uttering oracles that were often unsolicited and just as often unappreciated.

Over the centuries, the Church has understood the biblical prophets in a number of ways. They were seen as the high moral ethicists of the Old Testament. At other times, their contribution was to draw our attention to the Messiah, that is, Jesus Christ. At still other times, they were seen as the prosecutors who brought people's sins to light or religious reformers who led Israel to embrace monotheism.

MESSENGERS FROM GOD

Our modern understanding of biblical prophets changed dramatically with the 1933 discovery of ancient texts at an archaeological site in northern Syria. There French archaeologists uncovered an ancient library that was part of a little-known kingdom named Mari. The documents from Mari tell us a great deal about life in northern Mesopotamia along the Euphrates River in the eighteenth century BCE. Discovered among the documents was a collection of prophetic texts.

For the most part, the prophets described in these texts functioned at a shrine and provided the reigning king with oracles from their gods. But they could also function alone and in opposition to the king. More often than not, they brought from their gods a message the king did not want to hear. And even more important, the prophet would preface the message from the god by saying, "Thus says [the god's name]." The prophet would then speak in the first person narrative as if the prophet were the voice of this god speaking directly to his intended audience. In effect, the prophet was a messenger from the god to the king or some other official. When the prophet spoke, the god was speaking.

We find this same kind of "messenger speech" in several of the prophets of the Old Testament. For example, in Isaiah we read, "For thus says the Lord: I will extend prosperity to her like a river and the wealth of the nations like an overflowing stream..." (Isaiah 66:12). Notice how the prophet prepares his hearers for the message by using the formula, "Thus says the Lord," and then begins to deliver the message in first person narrative as if Yahweh were actually speaking. Here we see the prophet as a spokesperson or ambassador for Yahweh.

In ancient times, when the king sent an ambassador to deliver a message, he would tell the messenger exactly what he wanted to say, and the messenger would speak as if he were the king. Many times the king would empower the messenger to embellish the message, should unforeseen circumstances demand doing so. The messenger was more than just a mouthpiece; he spoke with the authority of the sender, and his audience knew it. A more modern example might explain what I mean.

Until the advent of headsets, a teenager's desire to listen to music often collided with a parent's desire to read the newspaper in peace and quiet. In countless homes across the country, a scene such as the following played out with regularity: Dad is in the living room trying to read the paper, while his teenage son is in the basement listening to rock music with the speakers at full tilt. Dad

hollers to the son to turn down the music, but the son can't hear the message. So Dad sends his youngest child to tell his brother to turn down the volume. The young messenger goes downstairs and tells his big brother to turn down the music. Big brother simply ignores his bothersome kid brother. Nothing happens.

A little while later, Dad is aware that the music has not come down in volume. He questions his youngest child. "I thought I told you to tell your brother to turn down the music," he says. Junior replies, "I did, but he wouldn't listen to me." Dad's face gets red, and he says to his son, "You go downstairs and tell your brother that *I said* to turn down the music."

Now the younger son has considerably more authority, and he goes downstairs to deliver the message with more confidence. He might even embellish the message a little bit for effect. If he were living in ancient times, his message might sound like this: "Thus says the father: Turn the music down. I am coming to you in a short while, and there will be great lamentation and wailing. The end is near. I am sorely grieved at your failure to obey. Turn the music down. The word of the father." The young son is acting as a prophet for his father.

This example underscores the reality of the biblical prophets: they came with a message and with the authority of the One who sent them. The intended audience might not like the message—and in most cases positively did not (see Jeremiah 38:1–6)—but that did not stop the prophets, even when it was dangerous to speak. The key to understanding the biblical prophets, then, is to realize that they were speaking a particular message to a very specific audience on behalf of God, who had sent them. Their words had divine authority whether their audience listened or not.

DID THE PROPHETS PREDICT THE FUTURE?

This understanding of biblical prophets raises some questions. Didn't the Old Testament prophets foretell the coming of Jesus and some of the events of his life? Certainly the prophets do speak of future events, but we must be careful not to lose sight of the basic function of biblical prophets. God called them at a specific moment in time to speak God's word to an audience living at that time. The prophet might announce a future event, such as a humiliating defeat by a hated enemy, but the prophet's focus was on the decisions that Israel needed to make in the present moment.

So when Isaiah spoke to King Ahaz about a sign of the future birth of a child (see Isaiah 7:14) or about a mysterious servant who will suffer for of the sins of many (see Isaiah 53:5), he was addressing a situation in his time, with a message for his contemporary audience. It is true that his words had a deeper meaning, which later Christians would read and understand. This meaning is what the Church has called *sensus plenior,* which means that Scripture can have a "fuller sense" that was not obvious at the time of the prophet. But if the prophet brings God's Word to a particular audience, we must approach it with an understanding of the prophet's own time and original audience.

The Israelites of the Old Testament saw reality in a way that was quite different from our modern American way of seeing things. For us, the future lies before us like a wide-open highway full of possibilities that we cannot yet see. The past lies behind us. We have moved on from the past and are heading straight into the future.

The Israelites would not have understood this image at all. For them, in fact, it was just the opposite. They had a word for "the future," but it was the same word for a human being's backside. And the word they used to describe "the past" was the same word they used to indicate what was right in front of one's face, one's front side. For them, the future lay *behind* a person; it could not be seen. And the past lay *before* a person; it was the only thing that person could see. So the Israelites would have perceived the human journey as "backing into the future."

In some ways, the Israelites' approach to the future was more realistic than ours. They could not tell the future any more than we can, because the future cannot be seen; it can only be derived. But that doesn't mean they had to stumble along an unknown path. What they could see was the past, the things that had happened, and the way God had worked in their lives up to that point. Had Israel been willing to listen to the prophets, they would have had good guides for moving into the future, but not because the prophets could see ahead. Instead they looked intently at their traditions, the experiences of the past, and the ways in which God had acted both graciously and destructively in their lives. From this vantage, it was not hard to "see" what would happen if people continued to disregard the covenant.

THE PROPHETS SPEAK TO US TODAY

Perhaps the best way to understand the biblical prophets is to view them as people of their own time who believed they were called to speak God's Word to that time. They were extraordinary individuals who could see deeply into their traditions in ways most of their contemporaries could not. They could see what was at the heart of Israel's continuing crises. They could not be silent. The words burned within them, and they had to proclaim, "Thus says the Lord."

The prophets' message put them at risk of being deported, imprisoned, or killed. The word they spoke had a power to "pluck up and to pull down...to build and to plant" (Jeremiah 1:10). The prophets challenge our comfortable assumptions about God. An article of faith among the Israelites was their belief they were God's Chosen People. Yet the prophet Amos reminded Israel that God had rescued the Philistines and the Arameans, two of Israel's hated enemies, just as God rescued Israel from Egypt (Amos 9:7). Amos was expelled from the kingdom of Israel for these words. But the prophetic word also built up and planted new seeds. The prophet Isaiah cried out to the Israelites, sunk in Babylonian exile for fifty years, "I am about to do a new thing...I will make a way in the wilderness" (Isaiah 43:19). God offered a new beginning when all hope was gone. To listen to the prophets is to risk imagining a new beginning when it is easier to remain defeated. Such is the dangerous power of the prophets' words. They spoke of empires long ago and promises long forgotten, but if we are willing to risk paying attention to what they said, we might find they speak to present empires and hopes yet to be fulfilled.

DISCUSSION QUESTIONS

1. *This chapter identified three general perceptions about the biblical prophets. Which one is closest to your own understanding of a prophet?*
2. *Using a Bible, make a list of the fifteen different prophetic books in the Old Testament. (Do not include the book of Daniel, for now.)*
3. *What was the major function of a biblical prophet?*
4. *In the ancient world, where might people find a prophet? (Hint: the chapter identified three possible settings.)*
5. *How did the prophets get their message? In other words, how did God communicate with them?*
6. *What does the author mean when he says that the Israelites saw life as "backing into the future?"*

FURTHER READING

Brueggemann, Walter. *The Prophetic Imagination*. Second Edition. Minneapolis, MN: Fortress Press, 2001.

Efird, James, M. *The Old Testament Prophets: Then and Now*. Eugene, OR: Wipf & Stock Publishers, 2001.

Leclerc, Thomas L. *Introduction to the Prophets: Their Stories, Sayings and Scrolls*. New York: Paulist Press, 2007.

Matthew, Victor H. *101 Questions and Answers on the Prophets of Israel*. New York: Paulist Press, 2007.

Ward, James M. *The Prophets* (Interpreting Biblical Text series). Nashville, TN: Abingdon Press, 1982.

CHAPTER 9
A New Approach to the Psalms: Embracing the Rhythm of Life

In biblical times, families and friends would sing psalms as they made their way to Jerusalem for yearly religious festivals. Jesus and his disciples sang some of the same hymns as they left the upper room after their last supper together. Today in monasteries and convents around the world, priests, nuns, and religious brothers gather at certain times of the day and night to pray the Psalms in a particular manner, guided by centuries of tradition. Lay women and men gather before morning Mass or set aside time alone to praise God with the words of those who lived more than two thousand years ago.

We might say the Psalms have great "staying power." Still, they come from a time and culture quite different from our own. How do we make sense of these prayers? Why do they echo, even now, some of our deepest yearnings and our strongest fears?

The Church has been fascinated with the Psalms for centuries. At one time, it was thought that King David wrote a majority of these prayers. The Jews in the Old Testament period remembered that before King David was a warrior, he was a musician and a poet in the court of King Saul. Long after his death, Jews continued to identify themselves with this popular king, waiting in hope for a "new David" who would restore their fortunes and their kingdom. When smaller collections of these psalms were copied onto scrolls, many of them were identified by the title instead of a number, for example: "a Psalm of David." Biblical scholars today, however, believe they were written by others who lived much later.

WHERE DID THE PSALMS COME FROM?

If David did not write the Psalms, then who did? The probable answer is that one person did not write the Psalms; rather, they developed out of the ongoing prayers of a faithful community. We naturally think of a song or poem as expressing the ideas and feelings of an individual. But in ancient Israel, a psalm grew out of the experience of a community. Indeed, these prayers were ultimately written down by individuals, but they could not claim to be the authors.

For centuries, scholars who studied the Psalms tried to find clues within them that would connect them to some particular event in the life of King David or the history of Israel. As in other parts of the Old Testament, the assumption was that the historical event would give meaning to the psalm. But these songs did not easily map to identifiable historical moments. Today this approach to studying the Psalms has been all but abandoned.

NEW WAYS TO STUDY THE PSALMS

In the nineteenth century, a German biblical scholar named Hermann Gunkel began to pay attention to the form of the Psalms. His extraordinary efforts have affected their study ever since. He observed that the Psalms could be categorized on the basis of their particular form. Most fell into one of three very different groups: the Psalms of Lament, which reflected an experience of sorrow or distress (for example, Psalms 3, 10, 22, 44); the Psalms of Thanksgiving, which breathed an enormous sigh of gratitude at being rescued from some danger (for example, Psalms 9, 18, 30, 32); and another smaller but important group of hymns that simply praised God, not just for what God has done, but for who God is (for example, Psalms 8, 100, 113, 150).

While scholars have identified many other forms within the Book of Psalms (penitential psalms, wisdom psalms, royal psalms, and so forth), it was Gunkel who recognized that the majority of the Psalms expressed great sorrow or great relief at the rescue from sorrow. Other biblical scholars have used that insight to look at the Psalms in a new way.

Walter Brueggemann, PhD, for example, has developed a way to bring the Psalms into our own personal lives. In his book titled, *Praying the Psalms,* he suggests that the Psalms reflect two very basic movements in everyone's life. One is the move into the "pit." It happens when our world collapses around us and we feel that there is no way out of the deep hole into which we have sunk. The other move is out of the pit into a welcome place. We suddenly understand what has happened and who has brought us up out of the pit.

Brueggemann further suggests that human beings regularly find themselves in one of three places: a place of *orientation,* in which everything makes sense in our lives; a place of *disorientation,* in which we feel we have sunk into the pit; and a place of *new orientation,* in which we realize that God has lifted us out of the pit, and we are in a new place full of gratitude and awareness about our lives and our God. Using these three "places," Brueggemann suggests that life has a rhythm as we move from one place to the next. He believes that the Psalms match those places and the surprisingly painful and joyful moves we make. In short, there are psalms of orientation, disorientation, and new orientation. Recognizing that different psalms match these three places in our lives can help us identify psalms that fit our personal lives.

PSALMS OF ORIENTATION

Psalms of orientation reflect the ordinariness of life. Most of us spend a large part of our lives in this place. Things are settled and life goes on a fairly predictable path. We have a sense of confidence in the regularity of life. Many of these psalms could be called "creation psalms," because they refer to orderliness and regularity of God's creation. Just as this world has a built-in structure to it, so too do our lives under the watchful care of God above (Psalm 33:13–15). We find in some of these psalms a sense that good people prosper and the wicked are punished. Psalm 112 extols the righteous for whom "wealth and riches are in their houses" (verse 3); their goodness makes them solid, like a rock, "secure in the Lord" (verses 6–7). Using many different themes and images, these psalms of orientation express the conviction that God is the one who guarantees life and protects it.

But life rarely stays so orderly and coherent; at times it can be brutal and irrational. We can watch our world collapse without warning, and we are pulled down into what seems a dark pit. In this place of disorientation hangs a great sense of abandonment. The psalmist moans, "My God, my God, why have you forsaken me?" (Psalm 22:1). Our usual response to this rupture of our equilibrium is denial. We want to believe that things are really okay, but even if we know they are not, we certainly do not want anyone else to know. Our denial forces us to cover up. We put on a happy face, and our isolation grows more intense.

PSALMS OF DISORIENTATION

A number of psalms give voice to experiences of abandonment in this broken and terrifying place long before the time of Christ. These lament psalms form the largest group of psalms in the Bible; they are audacious affirmations of faith. They bring this harsh brokenness to God, resisting the temptation to deny reality.

Those who prayed these laments were confident that God would understand their negative language. When we are in a time of disorientation, praying these psalms challenges our desire to keep up a good front and helps us bring to speech those feelings we might otherwise keep hidden. In one typical lament, the psalmist cries out four times, "How long?" and insists that God answer this prayer (see Psalm 13:1–3).

We may be uncomfortable with these prayers. How can faithful people speak to God that way? Yet they are the collective prayers of a people in pain. They are not magical, however; praying these psalms will not make everything better. But unless they are spoken, we run the risk of trivializing our relationship with God. The language of the lament calls upon God by name and expects a response. It takes a great faith to be so candid.

Every one of the lament psalms except Psalm 88 concludes with a prayer of thanksgiving. It would be simplistic to suppose that once the lament had been prayed, the person's complaint was immediately answered and life was restored. We do not know how many weeks, months, or even years passed before the psalmist could utter those words of thanks signaling the end of the lament. But concluding with a prayer of thanksgiving reflects our faith that God will rescue us and bring us up from the depths.

God does hear our prayer, and when this happens, it is a surprise which comes from the grace and goodness of God; the change in circumstances cannot be explained by logic or inevitability. The move to a new place in our lives, a "new orientation," as Dr. Brueggemann calls it, is accompanied by the language of joyful gratitude. We are fully conscious of this move as a gift. The Psalms of new orientation are filled with amazement, awe, and gratitude. They narrate how God has rescued the individual in a decisive way. Psalm 30 is a good example. The psalmist tells the story of sinking into the pit (see verses 8–10) and being raised out of it (see verses 11–12).

PSALMS OF NEW ORIENTATION

This period of new orientation is not simply a return to normal where everything is coherent again. The rhythm of life expressed in the Psalms is not circular. New orientation is another stage in our journey of faith. The experience of the pit has changed us, and the experience of God's grace has transformed our life. We cannot go back again. We now know something about life and God's way of fidelity that cannot permit a return to an earlier faith. The Psalms are not only personal prayers; they are above all "pilgrimage" prayers. Life becomes coherent once again, and the pilgrimage goes on.

The Psalms are prayers of praise that were spoken by individuals and by groups. They were sung in formal worship centers, such as the Temple in Jerusalem, though far more often in the private sanctuary of individual hearts. The psalmist sings: "Bless the Lord, O my soul, and do not forget all his benefits" (Psalm 103:2), then goes on to enumerate at least five of those benefits. Here we find a clue as to why the Psalms remained the prayer of a faithful community. We sing praise in order to remember because we so easily forget. These prayers remind us what it means to praise God, that is, to not forget all God's benefits.

CONCLUSION

When we pray the Psalms, we find in them the eloquence and honesty of a people who trusted that God was there in times of coherence, despair, and gracious gift. But we also bring to the Psalms our own similar experiences. We might express them in different and imaginative ways, but these ancient prayers still mirror our life struggles, and the pilgrimage of faith goes on.

Psalms for All Times and Seasons

Psalms of Orientation

These psalms reflect a very coherent picture of life. They describe how things are and should be; God made it that way. The world is a reliable place that provides rewards to the righteous and punishment to the wicked.

Psalms of Creation	**Wisdom Psalms**	**Psalms of Retribution**
Psalm 8	Psalm 14	Psalm 111
Psalm 33	Psalm 37	Psalm 112
Psalm 104		
Psalm 145		

Songs of the Torah	**Psalms of Well-Being**
Psalm 1	Psalm 131
Psalm 119	Psalm 133

Psalms of Disorientation

Life, however, is not always orderly; at times it is downright savage, broken and incomprehensible. The Bible contains a large number of psalms that are spoken from this void, but they are not full of despair. They are a witness that life must be lived as it really is, not in some pretend kind of way. The pits in one's life are mystifyingly real. Instead of stoic acceptance of these situations or, worse, a numbing denial, these psalms offer another approach: genuine lament.

Psalms of Personal Lament	**Laments from God's Side**	**Psalms of Sorrow**
Psalm 13	Psalm 50	Psalm 32
Psalm 35	Psalm 81	Psalm 51
Psalm 73		Psalm 130
Psalm 86		
Psalm 88		

Psalms of Community Lament
Psalm 74
Psalm 79
Psalm 137

Psalms of New Orientation

The songs of lament, characteristic of the prior stage of disorientation, end with a brief praise of God. It is not a "pre-paid" type of praise in which we pretend things will get better while stuck in the pit. Instead, something inexplicably new has happened which can only be acknowledged in joyful praise: laughing, crying, and thanking God, all in one unbounded act.

Thanksgiving Psalms	Hymns of Praise	Community Thanksgiving Psalms
Psalm 23	Psalm 1000	Psalm 27
Psalm 30	Psalm 103	Psalm 65
Psalm 34	Psalm 113	Psalm 66
Psalm 40	Psalm 117	Psalm 91
Psalm 138	Psalm 135	Psalm 124
	Psalm 146	
	Psalm 147	
	Psalm 148	
	Psalm 149	
	Psalm 150	

DISCUSSION QUESTIONS

1. *Did King David write the Psalms in the Bible?*

2. *What new approach did Hermann Gunkel bring to the study of the Psalms?*

3. *Of the three locations Dr. Brueggemann describes in his approach to the Psalms, where do you find you spend the most time? Would you add anything to the description presented here?*

4. *What are creation psalms? Do they tell us about how the world began or about the way we live our lives? Elaborate.*

5. *What is the largest group of psalms in the Bible? Why are there so many of this type of psalm?*

6. *Can you find the five attributes of God which Psalm 103 wants us to remember? (Hint: Psalm 103:3–5)*

7. *What is the main reason for praying the Psalms today?*

FURTHER READING

Brueggemann, Walter. *Spirituality of the Psalms*. Minneapolis, MN: Fortress Press, 2002.

Brueggemann, Walter. *Praying the Psalms*. Winona, MN: Saint Mary's Press, 1993.

Craghan, John F. *The Psalms: Prayers for the Ups, Downs and In-Betweens of life, A Literary-Experiential Approach*. Wilmington, DE: Michael Glazier, 1985.

Gunkel, Herman. *The Psalms: A Form-Critical Introduction*. Thomas M. Horner, trans.; Philadelpia: Fortress Press, 1967.

Harrington, Daniel J. *Why Do We Hope? Images in the Psalms*. Collegeville, MN: Liturgical Press, 2008.

Murphy, Roland E. *The Gift of the Psalms*. Peabody, MA: Hendrickson Publishers, 2000.

CHAPTER 10
The Wisdom Literature: Lessons About Life

In the Book of Jeremiah, we find one of those seemingly off-the-cuff remarks that tell us a great deal about Israelite society: "Then they said, 'Come, let us make plots against Jeremiah—for instruction shall not perish from the priest, nor counsel from the wise, nor the word from the prophet. Come, let us bring charges against him, and let us not heed any of his words'" (Jeremiah 18:18). In this short passage, we learn of the existence of three particular classes or offices in Israelite society, at least at the time of Jeremiah and presumably before. There were priests, who gave instruction; prophets, who spoke God's word; and sages, who gave counsel and advice. The priests and the prophets were most concerned about the covenant relationship with God, which was at the very center of Israel's faith. The sages, on the other hand, turned their attention to daily life in all its mystery. Over time, their advice and observations formed a wisdom tradition that captured another side of Israel's faith.

THE MEANING OF WISDOM IN THE BIBLE

We might think the word "wisdom" refers to the quantity of one's knowledge or to exceptional mental ability, but it meant more than that for Israel. In Hebrew, the word for wisdom was *hōkmâ*. Among its many possible meanings, it referred to the skill set of the artisan and the craftsman, for example, when Moses spoke of those who would create the furnishings for the house of God in the desert (Exodus 35:31). In this case, the word referred to a practical ability rather than a reservoir of facts. On another level, "wisdom" captured that sense of what was the appropriate thing to say and do in a given situation. This kind of demeanor could only be attained over time through countless encounters with the way things really were. On a third level, "wisdom" suggested a practical knowledge about how to get something done. In this sense, it was a skill set marked by common sense, which grew with experience.

Perhaps the common thread in these definitions is the emphasis on the amount of time it took to acquire these abilities. Wisdom was a cumulative endeavor; it grew over time within one who had the discipline and patience to nurture it. It was rare that someone young would be considered wise. The class of sages represented a movement within Israel to look deeper into the ordinary things of life and to find an order in the events that others had overlooked. In short, biblical wisdom discerned lessons about life from life.

But biblical wisdom was more than just the accumulation of a lifetime of experience; wisdom was also mysterious. It was present in the created world, inviting those who would listen to find the path to the place where wisdom dwelt. In the Book of Proverbs, the author described this experience as a lovely woman who called the young to follow the sound of her voice and find true wisdom; it was a wisdom that existed before creation and was now hidden within the created world (Proverbs 1:20–33; 8:1–21, 22–31). In the Book of Job, chapter 28 stands out as a separate meditation on the human search for wisdom. Ultimately God alone "knows its place" (28:23), and humans will have to search for it; but the author hints that "fear of the Lord" is the map that would guide them in this search.

Like Job, the Book of Proverbs announced the starting point

for the pursuit of wisdom: "The fear of the LORD is the beginning of knowledge" (1:7). However, it is important to note that "fear of the Lord" was just the beginning, not the goal, of wisdom. When the Hebrews encountered God on Mount Sinai, they drew back in terror (Exodus 19:16); the display of God's power was simply too much. And yet in the terror there was an attraction—they did not want God to leave. Their fear contained another side: a sense of enormous awe at something that was far beyond anything that human power could achieve. It is in the pull of these two forces— an overpowering fear and an enormous sense of awe—that the journey to wisdom's home began.

This wisdom tradition is found in five books in the Old Testament: Proverbs, Job, Ecclesiastes (Qoheleth), the Wisdom of Solomon, and Ecclesiasticus (Sirach). Anyone who reads any of these five books will immediately recognize a literary style quite different from the rest of the Old Testament. They are collections of proverbs, exhortations, meditations, dialogues, and instructions that reflect on hidden realities and invite deeper consideration such as, "The heart knows its own bitterness, and no stranger shares its joy" (Proverbs 14:10); and on generally self-evident intuitions such as, "What is crooked cannot be made straight" (Qoheleth 1:15). At times these sayings exhort the listener to action: "My child, perform your tasks with humility; then you will be loved by those who God accepts" (Sirach 3:17). Wisdom sayings usually are not arranged in any specific order, and the tone is very pragmatic.

The wisdom tradition in the Bible, however, was not just a collection of practical sayings and secular anecdotes. Biblical wisdom examined daily life to find the revelation of God that was unseen and underneath the ordinariness of daily events and in the perpetual problem of innocent suffering. This latter theme was the subject of the Book of Job; sometimes the divine order was at odds with Israel's own experience.

WHO WROTE THE BOOKS OF WISDOM?

This wisdom tradition did not develop in a vacuum, independent of Israel's covenant faith. Woven into these reflections were long-standing religious beliefs that were mandated by the Law and reinforced by the prophets: "Those who oppress the poor insult their Maker, but those who are kind to the needy honor him" (Proverbs 14:31); "The righteous will never be removed, but the wicked will not remain in the land" (Proverbs 10:30). In general, little reference was made to the usual covenant responsibilities such as worship, Temple sacrifices, religious festivals, dietary concerns, and laws regarding ritual purity. Nor did these books criticize society for its failure to keep the covenant, as did the prophets. They preferred instead to draw contrasts between the practical benefit of righteous living and the folly of its opposite. (See Proverbs 29:7.)

If this wisdom literature is so very distinct from the rest of the Old Testament, where did it come from? The question is not an easy one to answer. The name most often associated with wisdom is King Solomon. The Books of Proverbs, Ecclesiastes, and the Wisdom of Solomon all claimed him as author, but these books were written long after his reign. Scholars believe that Solomon's name was attached to these writings because of his reputation and place in Israel's history. In 1 Kings 3:9, Solomon's prayer for an "understanding mind" (literally, "a listening heart") is followed by the famous dispute over the identity of the real mother of a newborn child. (See 1 Kings 3:16–28.) Stories about Solomon were preserved because of his accomplishments. He built the Temple in Jerusalem and was known beyond the borders of Israel as fabulously wealthy. (See 1 Kings 10.)

Perhaps because wealth was considered a blessing of the wise, Jewish tradition credited thousands of proverbs and songs to him. But for someone so wise, Solomon also acted very foolishly. He took many foreign wives who turned his heart away from God and, in the end, God punished him for his disobedience by splitting his kingdom in two. (See 1 Kings 11.) Without a doubt, Solomon was a towering figure in Israelite history, but he was probably not the author of the books attributed to him.

THE ORIGIN OF ISRAEL'S WISDOM TRADITIONS

In the early nineteenth century, archaeologists unearthed thousands of documents from Egypt and Mesopotamia. Once they deciphered these texts, it became clear that Israel was not the only empire to have a wisdom tradition. Throughout the ancient Near East, each empire had texts that offered instructions, warnings, and reflections on daily life. Biblical scholars believe that Israel's wisdom tradition was part of a larger international tradition that existed throughout the ancient Near East. One indication of that larger picture is found in Proverbs 22:17—24:34. This particular collection is very similar to an Egyptian text called *The Wisdom of Amen-em-ope*. Who borrowed from whom can be argued, but the point remains that wisdom teaching was shared among the different cultures of the ancient Near East.

If Solomon is not responsible for the wisdom books in the Old Testament, then where did all these sayings, instructions, and proverbs come from? The question is hotly debated among biblical scholars; however, the wisdom literature itself provides some clues. The Book of Proverbs, for example, contains instructions and advice similar to what a parent might say to a child on any number of topics, for example, regarding laziness (19:15), lack of control of emotions (27:4), sexual impropriety (5:15–23), and the need for discipline and obedience (13:1, 24). Such instructions suggest the home or the larger clan was the source of this kind of wisdom.

Other proverbs and warnings seem more suited to public social behavior, such as controlling one's speech (13:3; 18:21; 25:15), avoiding public drunkenness (23:29–35), engaging in meaningful employment (14:23), and having good friends (17:9; 18:24). Such advice may have been part of a program of study for young men from families who wanted their sons to get ahead. These themes and many more may have formed the curriculum to prepare privileged youth for positions of authority in city life.

Still other proverbs concern the duties of the king and the work of the royal court: "A ruler who lacks understanding is a cruel oppressor; but one who hates unjust gain will enjoy a long life" (Proverbs 28:16). Observations like these would seem to point to the royal court as their place of origin. The Old Testament is full of references to advisers, counselors, and scribes at the royal court. Someone had to prepare the young princes for their duties as future rulers and diplomats. Perhaps the best that can be said is that Israel's wisdom tradition grew and developed in all three settings: the home, the school, and the royal palace.

WISDOM'S ALTERNATIVE PATH

In the last decades of the twentieth century, biblical scholars began to take a second look at these wisdom books in the Bible. Because there were so many connections with the wisdom writings of other cultures, many scholars treated these books as "imports." They were important for understanding cultural norms and expectations, but these texts were marginal for understanding the God of the Hebrews. But that evaluation has now changed; Israel's wisdom literature reveals another side of her faith in God.

Central to Israel's view was the belief in the mighty acts of God. The deliverance from Egyptian slavery, the victory over Canaanite armies, and the remarkable growth of the kingdom of David all testified to the power of God acting on Israel's behalf. But there was another reality in Israel's daily life: the deafening silence of God and the sense that God was far removed from the bewildering reversals in their life. If we have lived long enough, we all have had the experience of looking back at some event in our past in which we felt abandoned by God, only to see how truly graced that moment was. That is what wisdom theology knew and invited Israel to discover. God's presence is sometimes seen only in a "rear-view mirror": when we have moved far enough away from the event, then we see what God saw all along.

The sages believed in a hidden ordering to the universe and all things within it. With skill and experience, the wise person could fathom some of this order, but not all. There was also an inscrutable element in God's ways that could only be accepted, not plumbed: "The human mind may devise many plans, but it is the purpose of the LORD that will be established" (Proverbs 19:21). Not everything could be seen, no matter how much skill or experience one gained. God imposed limits on human nature, and some things could not be figured out. Humility, therefore, was another essential element in this pursuit of wisdom.

CONCLUSION

The wisdom tradition of the Old Testament teaches that much of ordinary life is lived in the experience of an invisible God; because of that fact, we might be tempted to believe that God is indifferent or angry and giving us the "silent treatment." But we would be foolish to do so. There is more going on in our lives than we see. The wisdom tradition of the Bible can guide us as we look deeper at our lives and our world than we are normally accustomed to doing. Without a doubt, our world is full of suffering and injustice, but it is equally full of promise and mystery. At the end of the creation story in Genesis 1, God gave the world a blessing and pronounced it "very good" (Genesis 1:28–30). The wisdom tradition found in the Old Testament never grew tired of exploring that mystery.

DISCUSSION QUESTIONS

1. *What were three distinct classes within Israelite life, and how did each group contribute to Israel's faith development?*
2. *What does the word "wisdom" mean in the Old Testament?*
3. *How does the Bible's definition of wisdom differ from modern day definitions?*
4. *What does the phrase "fear of the Lord" mean to you? What did it mean to the sages of Israel?*
5. *Where did all these sayings, proverbs, and teachings that comprise Israel's wisdom tradition come from?*
6. *Read 1 Kings 2—11 and make a list of things that show King Solomon's wisdom and things that show his folly. Which list is longer?*

FURTHER READING

Brown, William P. *Character in Crisis: A Fresh Approach to the Wisdom Literature of the Old Testament*. Grand Rapids, MI: Wm. B. Eerdmans Publishing Co., 1996.

Ceresko, Anthony R. *Introduction to Old Testament Wisdom: A Spirituality for Liberation*. Maryknoll, NY: Orbis Books, 1999.

Clifford, Richard J. *The Wisdom Literature*. Nashville, TN: Abingdon, 1998.

Murphy, Roland E. *The Tree of Life: An Exploration of Biblical Wisdom Literature*. Third Edition. Grand Rapids, MI: Wm. B. Eerdmans Publishing Co., 2002.

Murphy, Roland E. *Wisdom Literature & Psalms*. Nashville, TN: Abingdon, 1983.

CHAPTER 11

Is the End Near? Unraveling the Secrets of Apocalyptic Literature

In my first parish assignment, I regularly visited a dying parishioner. During his final days at home, he remained in the living room, the only space large enough to hold a hospital bed. On one visit, he was telling me about his family when the familiar sounds of a breaking news story came from the kitchen radio. My ear instinctively tuned in the radio, but the dying man kept right on talking, not even noticing the interruption. The events of this world no longer held any interest for him.

The Bible contains a small but important body of material that came from a mind-set similar to that of my dying parishioner. The name by which biblical scholars identify these books sounds ominous: *apocalyptic*. What exactly does this word mean? Why did some biblical authors choose to write this way? How can we understand what they are saying?

WHAT DOES THE WORD MEAN?

The term "apocalyptic" (from the noun form "apocalypse") comes from a Greek verb meaning "to reveal, pull back the curtain, uncover." In the Bible this term is applied to a body of writings that attempts to reveal, to a faithful remnant, something hidden from everyone else. The question could easily be asked: Isn't the whole Bible a revelation from God? The answer, of course, is yes; Christians believe the entire Bible is a revelation of who God is and who we are called to become. But the Bible uses a variety of literary forms in order to bring this revelation into our lives in a way we can understand and to which we can then respond, "I believe." One of those biblical literary forms is "apocalyptic," a special revelation characterized by a very distinct way of writing. Because these writings appear to describe the end of the world, few other passages in the Bible are so dramatic and so consistently misunderstood.

In the New Testament, the Book of Revelation clearly fits this type of writing. This literary form is also found in a few chapters in the Gospels (Matthew 24–25, Mark 13, and Luke 21), and Paul's very first letter contains some apocalyptic passages (1 Thessalonians 4–5). The Old Testament contains one complete apocalyptic book (Daniel) and several apocalyptic passages spread out within the prophetic books. The Book of Daniel is usually listed after the prophet Ezekiel in some Bibles, which is unfortunate. It gives the reader the impression that Daniel is a prophetic book. The Hebrew Bible does not place it with the prophets, but puts it instead in a separate section called "The Writings," along with Ruth, Esther, the Psalms and other such books.

Several prophetic books in the Old Testament contain apocalyptic sections. Isaiah 24—27 is often referred to as "The Little Apocalypse." The visions in Ezekiel 38—39, in Zechariah 9—14, and in parts of the Book of Joel are considered examples of apocalyptic writing in the Old Testament. But many other Jewish works that were written around the same time as these biblical books did not make it into the Hebrew Scriptures. The Book of Enoch, Jubilees, the Testament of the Twelve Patriarchs, as well as several distinct "apocalypses" attributed to various authoritative persons in Jewish history—Abraham, Ezra, Baruch and others—are just a few of the many apocalyptic writings that survived.

WHY DID THEY WRITE THIS WAY?

Perhaps the best way to understand apocalyptic writing is first to examine the mind-set of those who wrote in this way. If we look at the way these authors thought about life, their world, and the purpose of God in this world, then we can better understand the unique way in which they expressed their thoughts.

Two characteristics set apart the apocalyptic way of thinking: a sense of pessimism and a belief that events were moving toward a final point. For the most part, apocalyptic writers perceived a terrible world that was only getting worse. In most cases, they had good reason for such pessimism. The "faithful" were subjected to terrible persecution for their beliefs. Some Jewish groups responded to this persecution by engaging in guerilla warfare. Others, believing that they lived at a time when the power of the Evil One was cresting, deemed that approach useless.

Because evil in the world was so predominant and growing stronger, those who wrote apocalyptic literature saw their world reduced to two categories: good and evil. There was no in-between and no compromise. In this fundamental conflict, only God could successfully defeat the Evil One and destroy this evil world. Those who remained faithful to God would be victorious in the end, but for now they must wait in hope and continue to resist the onslaughts of the Evil One.

This mind-set reveals much about those who held it. First, they had no hope that things in their present environment would improve, either through active efforts to evangelize or by enacting social changes through political processes. They did not see this moment in time as temporary, a pendulum that would eventually swing the other way. They believed that society had already reached the "tipping point," to use an environmental expression with similar apocalyptic overtones, for this faithful remnant change would come only from a complete destruction of the existing world. Once this world was destroyed, then a new world could begin.

In some cases these apocalyptic communities separated themselves from their surroundings by physically moving to a new location. The residents of Qumran, for example, lived in a desolate location near the Dead Sea. Those who did not move physically did so spiritually. They distanced themselves from family and neighbors who, in their opinion, had accommodated this evil world. They saw themselves as "insiders," with the rest of the world on the outside. As insiders will often do, they developed a specialized language, with images and signs that were understandable to them but unintelligible to those on the outside.

This same mind-set produced a unique and vivid literature full of seemingly bizarre images and confusing references that described a cataclysmic destruction of this present world and an idyllic new world to come. The authors who wrote apocalyptic literature had many ways to express their thoughts, but the most common elements used in apocalyptic writing were dreams and visions. These were the normal channels through which God communicated to the Israelites. Some examples of this are Jacob's dream about the ladder leading up to heaven (see Genesis 28:12–17) and the angel's appearing to Joseph (see Matthew 2:13–14, 19–21).

In apocalyptic literature, the dreams and visions are shrouded in symbolic images and cryptic expressions. Animals and beasts play symbolic roles; numbers contain hidden bounty. The vision is often so unusual that it requires an angelic interpreter. Given that those who wrote this kind of literature viewed themselves as an oppressed minority living among hostile neighbors in an evil world, it is not surprising that the faithful few would resort to language only they could understand.

Because this community saw reality as a battlefield for the forces of good and evil, they described the final decisive moment as an all-out war between the power of evil and the power of

God. In such a battle, the outcome must be cataclysmic. Thus apocalyptic writings often become catalogs of catastrophes. In them we find descriptions of how the sun, moon, and stars will fall from the sky. Oceans will burst their boundaries, and mountains will crumble from unimaginable earthquakes. These images are often misunderstood in apocalyptic writing. The writers were not describing the way the world will end. They were using the theological language of Genesis when it describes the way the world returns to chaos in the story of Noah. (See Genesis 6–8.)

THE PURPOSE OF APOCALYPTIC LITERATURE

Many who read apocalyptic literature may believe that the writing does in fact predict the future. Isn't the purpose of apocalyptic writings to reveal when the world is going to end so that we may be prepared? The answer is no. God did not reveal the date of the end of the world to some ancient authors and tell them to hide that date so that every generation afterward would struggle to decipher it. Jesus even tells his disciples that no one knows that date, not the angels in heaven, not even the Son, but only the Father. (See Matthew 24:36.)

So what is the purpose of apocalyptic writing? There are two primary reasons for this kind of writing. Apocalyptic writing in the Bible was intended to strengthen waning faith in the midst of the chaos that surrounded a person or a community. Those who had taken God's words seriously and were trying to remain faithful could find themselves wondering if they were being foolish. Evil was increasing day by day, and those who compromised with the world seemed to prosper. But apocalyptic literature asserts first and foremost that God will be victorious in this struggle, as will those who remain faithful to God. The apocalyptic writer told his or her community—with veiled language to the outsider but with crystal clarity to the remnant—that God would win this battle. It would be a fearsome battle, but once it was over there would be no general amnesty, only victors and the vanquished. The time for making choices was now, but the time was short.

The nearness of the victory is the second reason for apocalyptic literature. It was meant to counter the fear that the end was a long way off and that no one would survive until then. Instead, several visions tried to encourage the faithful to hold on just a little bit longer because the end was very near. In the Book of Daniel, the visions of a succession of beasts or metals were meant for the insider, who knew these symbols stood for successive historical kingdoms. In each of the visions, the sacred writer emphasized that the present moment was in the last period before God's kingdom would be established. It was a way to interpret the present so that the faithful remnant would not lose hope.

The apocalyptic mind-set developed out of an overwhelming sense of desperation and frustration. Times of persecution are the breeding ground for the apocalyptic mind. It is not just that times are bad. Rather, the faithful few see absolutely no possibility that society is eventually going to get better. With desperation, they conclude that nothing will ever change. Tomorrow will not be a better day; it will just be more of the same. And with growing frustration they realize they are completely powerless to effect change.

It is not unheard of for the losing player in a game of chess or some other board game to suddenly knock all the pieces off the table, thus ending the game. Expressing the same frustration, the apocalyptic mind believes that God is going to wipe the slate clean. God will completely destroy this world and create a new one from scratch. The new world will not be a higher evolution of the present order, but a wholly new creation that can only be imagined or described in symbolic language. For the faithful, it will be complete and total vindication of their decision to remain faithful in the midst of crushing darkness.

CONCLUSION

Does apocalyptic literature have anything to say to us today? Many people would think we are in a new apocalyptic age. In past generations, the threat of nuclear war gave birth to all kinds of horrible predictions of the end of the world. Today concerns about global warming are doing the same thing. It would be easy to turn to the Bible and find all kinds of verses that "told us so." But apocalyptic literature was not concerned with how the world would end—not then, not now.

Apocalyptic literature was written to help people interpret the present, not the future. This biblical literature speaks to our present age in two ways. First the underlying premise of the apocalyptic mind-set is that God is actively involved in human history. What we might think is just the ongoing succession of events—sometimes surprising, most often routine—is not the way it really is. Everything is moving according to a divine drumbeat. Just because we do not see it does not mean God is not in complete control. Secondly, apocalyptic writing is filled with vivid images of cataclysmic conflicts. The images are intended to shake up our dulled senses and our complacency that we will not face our own end. The end is coming, not necessarily the end of the world, but the end of our world. Apocalyptic language is not intended to fill us with fear but to give us a sober sense of reality. Those who remained faithful to God were not afraid of the end, not because they knew the date, but because they knew the truth: the present age is always passing away. The apocalyptic writings keep this vision in focus.

DISCUSSION QUESTIONS

1. *What does the word* apocalyptic *mean to you? What does it mean to biblical scholars?*

2. *Name two books in the Bible that scholars generally agree are examples of apocalyptic writing.*

3. *Apocalyptic writing is said to inspire hope in its readers, yet this chapter suggests that apocalyptic writing comes out of a pessimistic mind-set. Is there a contradiction here?*

4. *Why do you think apocalyptic communities often separate themselves physically from the rest of society? Can you give any modern day examples of such separate groups?*

5. *Throughout history, just about every generation had some group that thought the world was going to end in their lifetime. Yet, it never does. Don't these failures invalidate the apocalyptic writings in the Bible?*

6. *Can you think of any visions from the Books of Daniel or Revelation that are particularly striking to you? Do you understand what they mean?*

7. *What does this chapter suggest is the purpose of apocalyptic writings?*

FURTHER READING

Carey, Greg. *Ultimate Things: An Introduction to Jewish and Christian Apocalyptic Literature.* St. Louis, MO: Chalice Press, 2005.

Collins, John J. *The Apocalyptic Imagination: An Introduction to Jewish Apocalyptic Literature.* Second Edition. Grand Rapids, MI: Wm. B. Eerdmans Publishing Co., 1998.

Cook, Stephen L. *The Apocalyptic Literature* (Interpreting Biblical Texts series). Nashville: Abingdon, 2003.

Russell, David S. *Prophecy and the Apocalyptic Dream: Protest and Promise.* Peabody, MA: Hendrickson, 1994.

Sneen, Donald J. *Visions of Hope: Apocalyptic Themes from Biblical Times.* Minneapolis: Augsburg Publishing House, 1978.

The Apocryphal Old Testament. Sparks, H. F. D., ed. New York: Oxford University Press, 1984.

PART THREE

Reading the
New Testament

CHAPTER 12
The World into Which Jesus Was Born

On the day Jesus was born, the world calendar did not suddenly reset, sending merchants and government bureaucrats in search of a calendar for the new era. In Jerusalem the year was 3760, at least for those scribes who kept records in the Temple; for the Romans, who were the latest overlords in this region, it was simply 754 *ab urbe condita* (from the date Rome was founded). It would be another five hundred years before the date of Jesus' birth would be reckoned the first year of our Lord (*anno Domini*).

THE *PAX ROMANA*

Decades before Jesus was born, the Roman Empire, which had steadily been consolidating its holdings and expanding its borders throughout the Mediterranean region, changed significantly. In 27 BCE, Octavian, the nephew of the assassinated Julius Caesar, took control of the Roman Empire and was promptly given a new name and title: Augustus *Imperator*; he would be the first in a long succession of emperors. He began a series of reforms that led to a two hundred year period known as the *pax Romana*: the Roman peace. He built superhighways across the empire, which allowed for the safe conduct of troops and the speedy transmission of information. He kept piracy in check on the Mediterranean so that commercial shipping could flourish. He held his provincial governors accountable for implementing a consistent rule of law throughout the empire. With these underpinnings, life in the empire could be quite tolerable. The borders were secure, new architecture and design made city life better, and newly built aqueducts brought fresh water, which improved health and life of citizens. In short, life in the Roman Empire was both a benefit and an imposition.

While Roman authors would describe the period around the time of Jesus' birth as a period of great peace, not all of her subjects would agree; to the Jews in Palestine, it was a time of simmering tensions. Like the Greek Empire two hundred years earlier, Rome ran up against a wall of resistance in Syria and Palestine, and as a result, the region was under tight Roman control. Both King Herod of Galilee and the Roman governor of Judea and Samaria knew they had two very specific tasks: to collect taxes for Rome's treasury and to keep the peace by whatever means necessary. For many Jews, the resulting greed and brutality on the part of the Roman occupation belied its claims of cultural and economic improvement. Rome's stunning achievements in language, government, law, engineering, and literature ran headlong into centuries-old and tested Jewish religious beliefs. The confrontation would prove disastrous to the Jews.

The presence of Roman legions posed a serious challenge to Jewish convictions that God had given this land to the Jews. For the past five hundred years, their land had been occupied by foreign rulers: first the Persians, then the Greeks, and now the Romans. The Jews struggled to understand why God had not driven out these foreign invaders. They wondered if they would ever be free to live in a kingdom of God's own making, like the kingdom of David and Solomon. As Jesus grew to manhood, he certainly knew this question had evoked several very different responses.

THE ORIGIN OF RELIGIOUS PARTIES IN JUDAISM

Two centuries before the time of Christ, the Greeks took over Palestine and sought to impose Greek education and culture. The story of the resistance they encountered is preserved in the Books of Maccabees. Against all political calculations, the Maccabees and their guerilla army defeated the larger and more powerful Greek forces in 164 BCE. The Maccabees, whose family name was Hasmoneus, established an independent Hasmonean kingdom for about a hundred years until Pompey and the Roman legions brought a severe dose of reality to this Jewish dream. The Hasmonean kingdom gave the Jews a brief taste of freedom in their own land; the return to foreign domination made the taste all that more bitter.

After the Maccabees won their war of independence, members of the established priestly family of Zaddok, which dated back to the time of Solomon, formed a new religious party. They tended to be from the wealthier side of Jewish life and had strong, conservative views about religion in the newly emergent Jewish kingdom. This group, known as the Sadducees, accepted the Torah (the first five books of the Old Testament) as their sacred Scriptures. Not surprisingly, the bulk of these Scriptures dealt with the kinds of sacrifices and regulations necessary for true worship. They did not believe in the resurrection of the body or the immortality of the human soul, since these ideas were not found in the Torah. They did believe that God only rarely intervened in human life. Instead God allowed humans to take the initiative and make the best out of their current situation. This rather temporal outlook helped them to be realists. When the Romans relieved the Hasmoneans of their rule over Judea, the Sadducees were savvy enough to know how to retain some power in the new political reality. Because they were the priests of the Temple, they already had a certain authority. As long as the Roman rulers would permit Temple worship and free observance of the Torah, the Sadducees were realistic enough to accommodate their new rulers and its culture. And Rome was only too happy to find a "reasonable voice" in the midst of so much hostility.

Another faction developed at the same time but went in a very different direction. They too were members of the prestigious priestly families in Judea, but they correctly saw that the Hasmonean rulers would not let the Temple priests operate with an independent authority. Before long the Hasmonean kings took over the role of the High Priest in order to consolidate their power. This interference in Temple worship was a blatant corruption of God's divine law and was the last straw for these loyal priests who may have been known at the time as the *hasidm*, "the pious ones."

This group became known as the Essenes; they believed that God was about to bring this irreversibly corrupt world to an end and create a new one where the law would be observed naturally, because it was inscribed on each person's heart (Jeremiah 31:33). For that reason, they chose to move out into the desert to prepare themselves for this coming kingdom through a life of strict observance of the law as God intended. The harsh conditions of the desert would serve as a test to purify their faith. They would not accommodate themselves to any foreign culture; they simply withdrew from it completely. While in the desert, their faith became more militant, and this desert community near the Dead Sea confidently prepared itself for the final cataclysmic battle.

Another group that came to exist after the Romans brought an end to Jewish independence was the Zealots. They wanted complete overthrow of the foreign domination of their land. Their heroes were the Maccabees, who had used guerrilla warfare to drive out the Greek rulers; if it had worked for the Maccabees in their fight against the Greeks, it would work again against the Romans. They believed that God had given the land to them, and it was their responsibility to reassert God's control over the land by opposing all efforts of the foreign occupation.

In 6 CE, when the Romans mandated a census to update the tax rolls, Judas, a Galilean, led an armed revolt that Rome put down harshly. Another Zealot, Theudas, tried to lead a large band of Jews across the Jordan River in a symbolic reenactment of Joshua's leading the Israelites into battle to take the Promised Land. The symbolism was not lost on Rome, and Theudas and his band of Zealots were executed. The execution of Zealots was always brutal and very public. The Roman governors wanted Jews to see the futility of revolt. For Zealots, however, these public executions simply inflamed the conscience of wavering Jews to join the Zealot ranks. At the heart of the Zealots' faith was the kingdom of God. They were not waiting for it to come; in their view, it already existed and they were removing the Roman pretenders. It was a struggle the Zealots would lose.

A more moderate group known as the Pharisees, whose name comes from the Hebrew word meaning "the separated ones," sought neither to accommodate nor to overthrow the hated Roman occupation. For the Pharisees, the laws in the Torah were central to their way of life. In this respect they were similar to the Sadducees. Unlike the Sadducees, however, they believed the laws had to be interpreted to apply to newer conditions. They put great emphasis on preserving their Jewish identity by strict adherence to the dietary restrictions of the law. In a very real sense, they separated themselves by living in a different way in the midst of the foreign culture. They were trying to establish a new identity for the Jews who lived in a predominantly alien culture. Because life was constantly changing, they believed that the Law had to be adapted to changing circumstances. Among the Pharisees, different rabbis had contrasting interpretations of how to observe the law. Even though the rabbis differed with one another, their argumentation and discussions permitted a vibrant observance of Judaism that was both practical and visible, as well as very popular.

EXPECTATIONS ABOUT THE KINGDOM OF GOD

All four of these Jewish sects had two things in common. First, they grew out of a reaction to the presence of foreign rulers in the land God had given to the Jews. Second, each had a distinct understanding of how God's kingdom, usurped by foreign rulers, would eventually be established. The Sadducees were the most realistic of the four groups. They accepted that God's rule was to be found in the system of sacrifices at the Temple under the control of their own high priest. They could live under foreign rule as long as the Temple cult was preserved.

The Zealots were the least realistic of all. They wanted complete freedom and the total defeat of all foreign occupiers. They believed that after they drove out all the foreign occupiers, God's reign would be complete.

The Essenes simply gave up on the present and looked to a time when God would make a new beginning. For them, the kingdom of God was coming, but only after a violent end to the present situation. God would do battle with the present kingdom of Satan, and in the victory, those who were faithful in the observance of the law would become the new Israel.

The Pharisees were perhaps the most idealistic. They believed that God's kingdom could grow in the present, as long as they remained separate from the corrupting influences of the foreign culture. Though they met regularly in synagogues to argue various opinions on how to keep the law, the Pharisees saw the home as the place where Jews would observe the law. Thus the home was the place where they could be separate from the culture while living in its midst.

Such was the world into which Jesus was born. As a Jew, Jesus would have shared many of the beliefs of that time. He grew up in Galilee, where Zealot feelings ran high. He certainly was exposed to all four of these expectations about the kingdom of God, but it does not appear that he aligned himself with any one of them. He too had an expectation about the kingdom of God; it formed the core of his preaching. (See Mark 1:15.) But this kingdom was not built on guerilla warfare, as the Zealots believed. When the soldiers came to arrest Jesus in the Garden of Olives, he made it clear that the sword had no place in the establishment of this kingdom. (See Luke 22:47–53.) At his trial before Pilate, Jesus was quite emphatic that God's kingdom did not need to be defended by troops. (See John 18:36.)

For Jesus, the kingdom of God was open to everyone, sinners as well as those who collaborated with the Romans by collecting taxes. Such a vision would have dismayed the Pharisees, who sought to draw strict lines regarding those who were on the inside and those who were outsiders. Jesus' justifiable anger at the way the Temple had been subverted from a house of prayer into a den of thieves must have put the Sadducees on notice as well. Jesus' exorcisms and healings were visible signs that the kingdom of Satan was coming to an end, not by an all-out battle between heaven and earth, as the Essenes believed, but by a humble submission to death on a cross.

CONCLUSION

In every way, Jesus' teaching would disappoint these various factions and in some cases provoke their unyielding opposition to his message. Why? For Jesus, the kingdom of God was not a replacement for the succession of kingdoms that come and go throughout time. The kingdom of God begins within the individual. It grows in the little daily choices we make to respond to others with love, to welcome others instead of judging them. It spreads rapidly, not by powerful preaching or political muscle, but by simple and sometimes heroic acts of kindness to one another. This radical approach began not in the corridors of power, but in a cave in Bethlehem of all places, and in a year that ever after would be considered year one.

DISCUSSION QUESTIONS

1. *If the Roman Empire brought so many improvements to a culture, why did Jews in Palestine resist the Roman occupation so strongly?*
2. *How did Roman presence challenge traditional Jewish beliefs about God's kingdom?*
3. *Who were the Hasmoneans, and what did they do that was so noteworthy?*
4. *Why did the Jews who moved out into the desert at Qumran exclude everyone else, including other Jews, from God's coming kingdom?*
5. *Why did the Pharisees believe in the resurrection of the body while the Sadducees did not?*
6. *How did Jesus' teachings disappoint each of the four groups discussed in this chapter?*

FURTHER READING

Fredriksen, Paula. *Jesus of Nazareth, King of the Jews: A Jewish Life and the Emergence of Christianity.* New York: Vintage Books, 2000.

Riches, John K. *The World of Jesus: First Century Judaism in Crisis.* New York: Cambridge University Press, 1990.

Saldarini, Anthony J. *Pharisees, Scribes and Sadducees in Palestinian Society.* Grand Rapids, MI: Wm. B. Eerdmans Publishing Co., 2001.

Wylen, Stephen M. *The Jews in the Time of Jesus: An Introduction.* New York: Paulist Press, 1995.

CHAPTER 13

How the Gospels Came to Be

In the recent past, the Gospels of the New Testament, and some that never made it into the Bible, were on the front page of most newspapers in the United States. Mel Gibson's movie, depicting the final hours of Jesus in all its gory detail, and Dan Brown's best selling novel, *The Da Vinci Code*, with its cleverly contrived clues to a modern day bloodline, left people wondering how Gibson and Brown got all that information from the four familiar Gospels that are read in church. We should take a closer look at what a gospel is and how the four Gospels came to be.

WHAT IS A GOSPEL?

Many people assume that the Gospels are biographies of Jesus Christ, and that is true to a point. They are biographies, but not like the ones you find in a bookstore today. As modern day biographies go, the Gospels are fairly incomplete. For example, they tell us nothing about Jesus as a youth or young man until his encounter with John the Baptist at the Jordan. Very little is written about Joseph, his foster father, and nothing is recorded about his extended family (grandparents, aunts, uncles, or cousins). Nor do we learn anything about his education or the work he did while growing up. We do not get an indication of who or what exerted the most influence on Jesus' life in his formative years or what lessons life taught him. These are the elements of any good biography today.

But the Gospels can be viewed as biographies if we understand what the people living in the first century CE understood as "biography." During the Roman era, there were many biographers: Plutach, Suetonius, and Tacitus to name some of the more famous authors. These biographers, however, worked with some limitations. It was rare that they could interview the subject of their biography. If the subject was dead, as was often the case, very little factual data was available. Instead they used a collection of stories passed down by those who may have known the subject. From this oral tradition and any documents that may have survived, the biographer would derive a sense of the person's character and personality. The biographer then arranged the stories and data in a chronological framework, which often contained large gaps because the biographer could not find pertinent information to complete the story.

This chronological framework was not intended to show the development or evolution of a person's character, as in modern biographies. The ancient authors believed that a person's character remained pretty much the same throughout life, and each succeeding event revealed that essential character in a new situation. People read biographies to be edified by the integrity of a person's character, not for the lessons they learned through the hard knocks of life.

The four Gospels are like these biographies up to a point. They have a chronological arrangement, and there are significant gaps in the life of Jesus. And like Greco-Roman biographies, the Jesus we meet at the Jordan River with John the Baptist is the same person we encounter in the Garden of Gethsemane. We do not find Jesus reflecting, towards the end of his ministry, on his successes and failures or what he learned from his ministry. What we find in each of the Gospels is a Jesus who exudes authority in every situation. He knows just what to say to those who challenge his teaching, he works miracles no one else can match, and he remains calm and composed throughout his trial. This quality of his character makes him and his teaching both a magnet and a lightning rod.

But there is a major difference between the Greco-Roman biographies and the four Gospels: Jesus rises from the dead. Though they share similarities with the form of a biography, they are not biographies in the modern sense. In fact, the New Testament has given them a special title: Gospel. The Greek word for gospel is *euangelion*; it became *evangelium* in Latin, and English dubbed the person who put the *evangelium* into writing an evangelist. But the original word literally means "good news that is proclaimed to an audience." In the Roman Empire, some great accomplishment of the emperor would often be proclaimed in the towns and villages of the Empire by messengers sent with this important evangelium.

Two things are important to understand about this term "gospel." It referred to news that was perceived as *good* to those who heard it proclaimed for the first time. And it evoked some kind of personal response from the one who heard it. So both the way the news was proclaimed and the way it was heard were extremely important. What we have in our Bibles today is the written form of that proclamation, a form that is something like a biography. But underlying that written form was a spoken proclamation that generated an amazing response in faith in those first hearers. Today I may not respond in amazement when I hear a Gospel read in church or in my own private study, but the invitation to respond is still the same. I may be convinced that my sins have eliminated any possibility of eternal life, and then I read, "Has no one condemned you?...Neither do I condemn you" (John 8:10–11), and in my heart, I have new hope to try again. Or maybe I am feeling pretty smug about my virtuous way of life, and I hear Jesus say, "All who exalt themselves will be humbled, and those who humble themselves will be exalted" (Luke 14:11);

I resolve to be more understanding and less judgmental of others. These are the appropriate responses to the Gospel that I have just heard. Biographies in antiquity may have edified those who read them, but the Gospels in the New Testament encouraged a change of heart.

HOW DID THE GOSPELS COME TO BE WRITTEN?

In order to listen intelligently to the Gospels today, we have to know how they went from being a preached word to a written one. Perhaps the easiest way to understand that process is to divide the first century of the Christian era into three parts. Each period (roughly thirty years) contributed to the formation of the four Gospels in the New Testament. The first period included the time of Jesus' public ministry. During this time Jesus gathered disciples, taught them, worked powerful miracles, and sent his disciples out to proclaim that the kingdom of God was at hand.

At the end of this period, while Pontius Pilate was procurator of Judea (26–36 CE), Jesus was crucified and rose from the dead. His resurrection changed everything. Now his disciples began to understand what Jesus had told them. His promise of eternal life was powerful good news, backed up by his own resurrection. Of course, not everyone believed that Jesus had risen from the dead. Although the tomb was empty, not everyone believed Jesus had risen from it. But his disciples did believe, and so began the second stage in the formation of the Gospels.

During this second period (30–70 CE), the Apostles, other disciples, and Paul began preaching. They had a powerful message to spread: the good news that death was not the end. The kingdom of God began here on earth, but was to be fully enjoyed only after death. The poor, the outcast, the sinners, and the marginalized all had access to the kingdom of heaven. And there was an added urgency to this missionary activity. They believed that Jesus would return soon. At that time, he would bring an end to this world and pass judgment on the wicked; all the faithful who believed in Jesus would be led into God's eternal kingdom.

For Christian missionaries in this second part of the first century, there was no time to lose. The Apostles went from city to city, speaking first to Jews, then more and more directly to gentiles. Those who believed formed communities that would gather in the home of one of their members after Sabbath and celebrate Eucharist. If one of the Apostles was present at these gatherings, he would tell stories about what Jesus had said and done.

The purpose of telling these stories about Jesus was to encourage Christians in their own trials and difficulties. Many times the preachers would address local problems in the community by telling them how Jesus had handled similar situations. Rather than tell the assembly everything Jesus did, they tailored their good news to what the audience needed to hear. As the Apostles traveled from region to region, some stories were told in one place and other stories in another. They were not trying to tell the whole life of Christ, but just the pieces that applied to their audience at a particular moment. Uppermost in their preaching was the hope that listeners would come to believe in Jesus as Lord and Savior and change their lifestyle to conform to his teaching.

But by the mid sixties, a new reality was becoming apparent. Jesus was not returning as soon as they had originally thought. Christian communities needed to restructure themselves in order to maintain and develop the faith of its members. There was a need to preserve the traditions about Jesus and his teachings in writing, since those who had been with him during his earthly ministry were now dying or being killed. The third and final stage (70–100 CE) in the formation of the Gospels now began. Certain individuals in various Christian communities throughout the Mediterranean took the "good news" they had heard and wrote it down in an orderly sequence for their own community. (See Luke 1:1–3.) Tradition would call these individuals evangelists, because they preserved in written form the *evangelium*, that is, the Good News of Jesus Christ.

FOUR PORTRAITS OF JESUS

One of the first persons to compose a Gospel was a man traditionally known as Mark. Although Mark's Gospel is the shortest, his work rendered an enormous service to Christians everywhere. It is believed that he composed this account just after the Romans destroyed Jerusalem in 70 CE. He may have written his Gospel in Rome. His document was copied and recopied and made its way around the Roman Empire. In Antioch, Ephesus, and perhaps even in Greece, other individuals began to compose gospels for their communities. Using Mark as a source, they added other stories and words of Jesus that they recalled from their local communities. Though many individuals in many places wrote gospels, only four were finally accepted by the early Christian community as authoritative and inspired. These become known as the Gospels of Matthew, Mark, Luke, and John.

Each evangelist chose to emphasize a particular characteristic of Jesus that captured the imagination and faith of his own particular community. Mark's Gospel emphasizes the impact of the cross on the disciples' lives, while Matthew focuses on Jesus' Jewish roots and his appeal to gentiles. Luke emphasizes the compassion and care Jesus had for the poor. And John, the latest of the four Gospels, paints a majestic portrait of Jesus, fully divine, with the words of eternal life for all who believe.

CONCLUSION

What makes the four Gospels distinct from the biographies of antiquity is that they are not about some person in the past whose life and character give us a noble model to admire. The Gospels are the words and deeds of a living Person today. It is true that the words were spoken in a culture far different than ours. We need to develop reliable methods to study these texts to hear them correctly. But it is worth the time and effort to do so, because the words of that living Person are still "Good News" today.

DISCUSSION QUESTIONS

1. *What was your impression of the Gospels in the New Testament before you read this chapter? Has your impression changed after reading the chapter?*
2. *How is a biography written during the time of the Roman Empire different from a biography written today?*
3. *Can you think of any examples in the four Gospels where Jesus' authority is clearly evident? What was the response of people to his authority?*
4. *Why are there four Gospels in the New Testament? Wouldn't one Gospel be enough?*
5. *What is your favorite Gospel and why?*
6. *How does the comparison of the Gospels with a painted portrait help explain the nature and purpose of a Gospel?*

FURTHER READING

Burridge, Richard A. *Four Gospels, One Jesus? A Symbolic Reading.* Second revised edition. Grand Rapids, MI: William B. Eerdmans Publishing Co., 2005.

Catchpole, David R. *Jesus People: The Historical Jesus and the Beginnings of Community.* Grand Rapids, MI: Baker Academic, 2006.

Marsh, Clive and Steve Moyise. *Jesus and the Gospels.* New York: T & T Clark International, 2006.

Nickle, Keith Fullerton. *The Synoptic Gospels: An Introduction.* Revised and expanded edition. Louisville, KY: Westminster John Knox Press, 2001.

Senior, Donald. *Jesus: A Gospel Portrait.* Revised and expanded edition. New York: Paulist Press, 1992.

CHAPTER 14
Acts of the Apostles: Its Purpose and Message

A cts of the Apostles is often called the "Gospel of the Church" or the "Gospel of the Holy Spirit." In some ways these monikers are appropriate in that the four Gospels tell the story of Jesus, and Acts tells the story of how the Spirit guided the growth of the Christian church. But Acts of the Apostles is more than a narrative of events in those early years after Jesus ascended to heaven; reading Acts of the Apostles for the first time does something to the reader. Some readers wish they could go back to that golden period when there was a wonderful harmony and generosity among the believers; others are thrilled and edified by the stories of the early apostles and the courage of the martyrs. Clearly Acts of the Apostles is an exceptionally well written and exciting narrative that accomplishes exactly what its author intended. Those who want to read it with a deeper understanding and greater appreciation must be willing to take a closer look at that author, the work he produced, and his intention.

WHO WROTE ACTS?

The Gospel of Luke and Acts of the Apostles were written by the same author. Each book has a short preface in which a patron, perhaps, is identified as Theophilus. The final scene in the Gospel, the ascension of Jesus (Luke 24:50–53) becomes the first scene in Acts (Acts 1:6–11). Several literary parallels between the two works indicate a single author for both. Biblical scholarship is almost unanimous on the issue of one author for both works. But who is that author?

Early Church tradition identified that person as Luke. One of the earliest papyrus manuscripts of the four Gospels identifies Luke as the author of the third Gospel; this manuscript, called P75, is dated between 175 and 225 CE. Both Irenaeus (c. 12–202 CE) and Tertullian (155–222 CE) accepted this identification and spoke of Luke as a physician and companion of Paul, based on three references to a "Luke" in Paul's letters (Philemon 24; Colossians 4:14; and 2 Timothy 4:11). Irenaeus and others made the connection between the Luke mentioned in Paul's letters and the Luke of the Gospel and Acts, because Paul dominated in the story of Acts, and there are several "we passages" in Acts.

These "we passages" appear when Paul begins a new missionary effort among the Greeks, and the narrator now becomes a participant in the story: "When he (Paul) had seen the vision, *we* immediately tried to cross over to Macedonia, being convinced that God had called *us* to proclaim the good news to them" (Acts 16:10). Biblical scholars, however, have doubts about the authenticity of these narratives. Are they inserted into the story from a "travel diary" maintained by Luke while accompanying Paul? If so, why do they seem to start and stop, leaving large gaps in the first person narrative? Could it be that Luke acquired someone else's travel diary and used parts of it to add interest to his account? Or did the author simply create them in imitation of other well-known Greek narratives similar to Acts? In short, scholars today are not as convinced as Irenaeus that these special passages prove the author of Acts was a traveling companion mentioned in Paul's letters.

Another reason why some biblical scholars doubt the author of Acts is the coworker and companion of Paul stems from troubling discrepancies between the picture of Paul in Acts and the one we get from Paul's own letters. An example of this discrepancy concerns what has become known today as the "Council of Jerusalem" described in Acts 15. In the account, Paul and Barnabas go to Jerusalem to discuss the requirements for gentiles who convert to the Christian way. At the meeting, it was decided that male gentiles did not need to be circumcised, and gentile converts did not need to follow the Jewish dietary laws except in cases of food sacrificed to idols or with the animal's blood still in it. We are told this decision had the complete support of the whole church (Acts 15:22). But when Paul wrote to the Galatian community because they were being misled by Jewish Christians who claimed that gentiles must be circumcised, he did not mention this "decree" from the council in Jerusalem (Galatians 2:6–10). And in 1 Corinthians 8, when Paul talked about eating food sacrificed to idols, he never mentioned the decision. Apparently Paul never knew about this decision or was informed about it only at the end of his missionary travels (Acts 21:25). Or perhaps Luke created the narrative of a unifying council that recognized the mission of Peter to the Jews and Paul to the gentiles for another purpose.

Given the discrepancies between the Paul in Acts and the one we find in his own letters, it does seem questionable whether this Luke was the traveling companion and coworker of Paul. Luke was a common name, and there could have been more than one Luke who converted to Christianity. It is perhaps better to regard this Luke as a separate Christian whose gift to the early Christian church was a two-volume work of inestimable value. But from that work there are some things we can know about this Luke. He was well educated and used a large vocabulary as well as a better Greek style in his writing. He also has a good knowledge of the local customs and titles used to identify "officials" in the various cities and towns that Paul visited. And he knew how to write a very good story that would keep the audience's attention while challenging their faith. This persuasive writing style may be the most important thing we need to know about him.

WHAT KIND OF BOOK IS IT ANYWAY?

Most readers assume that Acts of the Apostles is a history of the early days of the church. But the title given to the book in the early tradition is "Acts," which in Greek refers to the glorious deeds of notable persons like kings and military heroes. Certainly Acts of the Apostles contains its share of dramatic episodes about apostles who won't stay put in prison or who perform dangerous exorcisms and even raise the dead to life. In these and many other stories like them, the author cloaks a "lesson" with humor, surprise, excitement, and bravado. In a certain sense, the Acts of the Apostles encourages similar "acts" of witness and faith from its audience.

Still most people think of Acts as history. And that is probably closer to what the author intended to write. In the prologue to the Gospel of Luke, the author said he wanted to provide Theophilus with an "orderly account" of the extraordinary events that took place. Luke wrote history as it was written in antiquity. He used sources for his work where they existed, and he filled in gaps by creating speeches for his character. These twenty-eight speeches make up almost one-third of the entire book of Acts. Creating speeches for important occasions was common in Greek and Roman histories. The art of the historian was shown in the way he composed the speech to fit the story and the speaker and, at the same time, interpret the significance of an event. Luke simply followed the rules of historical writing for his day; the speeches revealed how the early church understood the meaning of what Jesus did and God's plan for the church.

WHY ACTS OF THE APOSTLES?

The Gospel of Luke is the only Gospel to have a sequel. Why didn't any of the other Gospels have one? For Luke, the story of Jesus did not end with his death and resurrection. Something new has begun in the history of the world. Luke wants his own generation to see what has begun and what it means for them. There are surely many reasons why Luke wrote Acts; I would like to suggest two.

One of Acts' strongest and most enduring images is the picture of the early Christian community. Short summaries of life in the early church are scattered throughout the first part of the book; other transitional verses in the book function as brief summary reflections. The larger summaries give a very positive picture of the Christian faith; there is a strong bond of unity and material support among the Christians. The picture, of course, is meant to portray an *ideal* time. The letters of Paul make it clear that there were many divisions within the early Christian communities. But Luke deliberately fashions an ideal picture to help his own community, living perhaps forty years after the time of Jesus, to find its own path through that very difficult period when Christianity and Judaism separated for good. One could say that the whole book of Acts is ideal, in some ways. The growth of the church is incredible, and its members are gifted with the ability to perform miraculous deeds and preach powerful sermons about Jesus. More than simply telling us what happened, Luke invites us to reconsider what God did and continues to do in the community of believers.

Related to this ideal picture is the way Acts of the Apostles tries to strengthen the faith of Luke's own community; it is a community that yearns for that ideal time as it goes through the confusing and painful time after Rome destroyed Jerusalem. In 66 CE, Jews in Palestine revolted against Rome's control of Palestine. It was a disastrous miscalculation; the Roman army harshly suppressed the rebellion, and in the process, destroyed Jerusalem and the Temple. It was a devastating defeat for the Jews. By 80 CE, the relationship between Jews and Jewish Christians had been irreparably broken. Jewish Christians now looked to an uncertain future in an increasingly gentile Christian church. Was God at work in all of this? Luke's second volume answers with a resounding "yes." God is working through the guidance of the Holy Spirit. Right from the very beginning, the gift and guidance of the Holy Spirit took people by surprise: they were surprised at the gifts of speech and healing at Pentecost and beyond. They were surprised at the wisdom coming out of the mouths of ordinary fishermen, whose simple eloquence confounded the Jewish authorities. But they were in for the greatest surprise of all: the conversion of a young Jewish Pharisee, intent on eliminating this blasphemous splinter group, who became its most powerful champion and missionary. Whether Luke knew Paul personally or not, his work provides an important framework for reading his letters and understanding Paul's impact.

DISCUSSION QUESTIONS

1. *If you have read Acts of the Apostles or heard it read in church, share any stories from it that you remember. Why did you remember that particular story?*
2. *Look up the three places mentioned in this chapter where Paul tells us something about Luke. What exactly does he say about Luke?*
3. *Why did the early church fathers like Irenaeus and Tertullian connect Luke (from question #2 above) with the author of Acts of the Apostles?*
4. *Many scholars believe that the speeches in Acts of the Apostles are not transcripts of actual speeches, but rather were composed by Luke for another purpose. Why wouldn't that have surprised Luke's audience?*
5. *If things were not as positive and ideal as Luke described in the early chapters of Acts, why did he say they were? Isn't that deceitful?*

6. *Why did Luke write the Acts of the Apostles? How does it still apply to our lives today?*

FURTHER READING

Crowe, Jerome. *From Jerusalem to Antioch: The Gospel across Cultures.* Collegeville, MN: Liturgical Press, 1997.

Doohan, Leonard. *Acts of Apostles: Building Faith Communities—A Spiritual Commentary.* San Jose, CA: Resource Publications, 1994.

Jervell, Jacob. *The Theology of the Acts of the Apostles.* New York: Cambridge University Press, 1996.

Johnson, Luke Timothy. *The Acts of the Apostles.* Collegeville, MN: Liturgical Press, 2006.

Pilch, John J. *Visions and Healings in the Acts of the Apostles: How the Early Believers Experienced God.* Collegeville, MN: Liturgical Press, 2004.

CHAPTER 15
The World of Paul and His Letters

Saying that Saint Paul was important in the early Christian church would be a gross understatement. One way to look at his influence is to examine the table of contents of the New Testament. Of the twenty-seven books, just about half (thirteen) are letters that claim to be written by Paul. In addition to these letters, the majority of Acts of the Apostles is about Paul. From a modern public relations point of view, one might conclude that Paul had a very good agent indeed!

By many estimates, Paul is responsible for the spread of Christianity out of the local communities in Jerusalem and into many of the major cities of the Roman Empire well before the end of the first century. He paved the way for Christianity to emerge from its Jewish roots with his strong conviction that gentiles could find salvation without first adopting core Jewish practices. Paul's letters also give a snapshot of the earliest Christian community with all its enthusiasm and confusion about the meaning of Jesus' death and resurrection. There is an urgency in Paul's preaching, perhaps because he was convinced Jesus would soon return. Through the eyes of Paul, we get to see how the first Christians came to believe in Jesus and what that belief meant for them. If Pentecost is considered the "birth" of the church, then in Pauline letters, we see the early Christian church taking its first steps and learning to walk.

WHO WAS PAUL?

Given the number of books in the New Testament associated with Paul, one would think we have a lot of information about him. However, that is not the case. Our largest source of biographical information comes from the Acts of the Apostles. But when scholars examined the stories about Paul in Acts, they noticed that the image there did not always agree with the picture of Paul in his letters. Still Acts of the Apostles can offer us a framework from which to view Paul's life, especially the different missionary journeys he undertook. When trying to get a picture of the "real" Paul, we have to keep asking ourselves where our information comes from. Today scholars give priority to what Paul said about himself and weigh carefully what is found in Acts.

From his letters, it seems Paul viewed his life in three stages: as a Pharisee before his conversion, during his conversion experience, and finally, his activities as an apostle and minister of Christ. Acts of the Apostles fills in this brief outline and offers us a sequential arrangement of Paul's travels, but one must be cautious here. Luke had a larger theological purpose than simply providing a life of Saint Paul.

From Paul himself we learn that before his conversion, he could boast of his genuine Jewish credentials. He was a Hebrew and a member of the tribe of Benjamin, circumcised soon after birth in conformity to the law. He became a Pharisee, zealous in upholding that same law (Philemon 3:5). Quickly that zeal translated into persecution of those Jews who believed Jesus was the Messiah (Philemon 3:6).

Paul's conversion was the defining moment of his life. It is hard to know what actually occurred in his conversion experience. Luke retells the event three times in Acts of the Apostles (9:1–22; 22:4–16; 26:9–18). But in his letters, Paul does not give any description of the event— concentrating instead on its meaning. For him it was a vision for the risen Lord (1 Corinthians

9:1) and a revelation (Galatians 1:12) in which Paul was given to understand the meaning of Jesus' death and resurrection. Most of us are captivated by the dramatic details found in one of the accounts in Acts and focus on the marvelous "conversion" that took place. But Paul himself only briefly acknowledges the surprising grace of Christ in his conversion (1 Corinthians 15:8–10). Paul interprets this event in much the same way the prophets of the Old Testament understood their own vocation. Though Paul had not realized it, God had chosen him even before his birth, like the prophet Jeremiah (see Jeremiah 1:4–10), to be an apostle to the gentiles (Galatians 1:16).

During his years as a zealous missionary, Paul emphasized that he was a true Apostle, like the others whom Jesus appointed; he even challenged Peter in a dispute in Antioch (Galatians 2:11–14). He spoke about his early travels in Cilicia and Syria (Galatians 1:21) and his work in many of the major cities throughout Asia Minor and Greece. Paul alluded to a physical infirmity that burdened him, though he never said what it was (Galatians 4:13–14; 2 Corinthians 12:7–8). It appears that Paul did not see himself as a good preacher (2 Corinthians 10:10; 11:5–6). He also told his readers about the cost of believing in Jesus: his sense of rejection by his fellow Jews (Romans 9:1–5), his sufferings, the dangers he constantly faced in his travels, and his imprisonment in service of the Gospel (1 Thessalonians 2:2, 15; 2 Corinthians 6:4–5). Acts of the Apostles gives us a far more captivating account of Paul's life, but it is in Paul's letters that we find the soul of this extraordinary apostle and the conviction that all this colorful detail was unimportant in the light of what Christ offered.

THE LETTERS OF PAUL

The New Testament contains thirteen letters attributed to Paul. In the first Christian centuries, the Church fathers also believed Paul wrote the Epistle to the Hebrews, but modern scholarship almost unanimously rejects that opinion. Paul most certainly wrote other letters, some of which may have been edited and combined with known letters, for example, in 1 & 2 Corinthians. Some were lost, like the letter to the Laodiceans mentioned in Colossians 4:16.

Biblical scholars today divide this collection of letters into three groups. The first group is called the genuine or "undisputed" letters of Paul. Virtually all New Testament scholars believe Paul wrote these seven letters. They share a similar vocabulary and have a common grammatical style and, with the help of Acts of the Apostles, they can be assigned a rough chronological sequence. The earliest letter, 1 Thessalonians, was most likely written around 50–51 CE. If Paul's prophetic call/conversion experience took place around 35 CE, then Paul spent at least fifteen years preaching about Jesus and dealing with the faith formation of his communities before this letter was written. Paul may have written other letters before this one, but if he did, they were not preserved.

The second group of letters is sometimes referred to as the "doubtfully genuine" letters of Paul, or the Deutero-Pauline letters, a term which implies the letters came from a close disciple of Paul. The vocabulary, style of writing, and theological ideas are slightly different from the seven genuine letters of Paul. Some authors suggest that the style and vocabulary differences could be explained if, perhaps, Paul had simply outlined his ideas to a scribe who then wrote them down, with Paul later giving final approval.

The final group of letters is called "the pastoral letters." Scholars do not know who wrote them, but they do not believe it was Paul. Important Pauline themes such as faith, righteousness, and law are treated in a different way than in the seven genuine letters. It is believed that the author is deliberately appealing to Paul's authority to deal with a new situation in late first century or early second century. The rapid growth of Christians required a more developed inner structure to the Christian community and a different way to respond to hostile forces opposing the Christian churches.

Another element that may affect one's decision on the question of authorship is the presupposition that Paul did not write his letters himself. Since the late 1800s, scholars have had access to a large collection of Greek papyri found in Egypt. These texts indicated that a secretary was often used in the writing of letters; Paul's genuine letters seem to substantiate this practice. At the conclusion of the letter to the Romans, there is a greeting from the secretary: "I Tertius, the writer of this letter, greet you in the Lord" (Romans 16:22). Sometimes Paul told his audience that he was writing the final greeting himself, implying that someone else wrote the main part of the letter (see 1 Corinthians 16:21). He alerts the Galatians to his own hand in the letter, which is in a noticeably larger script (Galatians 6:11). Paul may have used his trusted companions as scribes for his letters, which may explain his mention of Timothy and Silvanus in the greetings of many of his letters. What is unknown is whether Paul dictated his letters word-for-word. He may have simply talked out the problems he wanted to address with his companions and let them or a professional scribe compose the letter, with Paul having final approval before it was sent. If Paul did not use the same secretary for all his letters, that might explain why a different grammatical style is found in some of the disputed letters.

HOW TO READ A LETTER FROM PAUL

If we accept the division of the thirteen letters attributed to Paul as suggested above, then one of the implications is that we should form our perceptions of Paul based on his seven "genuine" letters. It is also helpful to remember that these letters were written primarily to address specific problems within a community that Paul himself founded. He writes to answer their questions, encourage their faith, and to correct false teachings that are developing in his absence. So when reading a Pauline letter, it is necessary to understand the problem that prompted the letter in the first place.

We should also pay attention to the *way* Paul wrote his letters. Paul's letter to Philemon is an example of a very personal letter; his letter to the Romans, a community which Paul did not establish, is more formal. Because so many letters have survived from the Greco-Roman world, we have a clearer idea of the many forms that a letter could take and the different parts that made up a letter. In all of Paul's letters, except for Philemon, Paul follows a basic format. First, a *greeting* indicates the names of the sender and the addressee. It is followed by an expression of *thanksgiving*. The *body* of the letter contains Paul's central message, which addresses the problem in the community. Here Paul uses different forms of argument or persuasion and usually concludes by encouraging faith and making suggestions about behavior. The *conclusion* of the letter combines a final greeting and a brief benediction. Paul often greets people in the community by name or passes on the greetings of others to the community.

In Paul's first letter, 1 Thessalonians, the "thanksgiving" part of the letter is quite noticeably extended (1 Thessalonians 1:2–3:13). Such a lengthy thanksgiving is unusual, and it alerts us to the gratitude Paul feels for the Thessalonians. Once we notice this change to the usual form of a letter, we begin to hear the depth of feeling Paul is expressing. In the same way, when reading the Letter to the Galatians, we should notice there is no "thanksgiving" part to the letter at all. Paul is not thankful for the way the Galatians are having second thoughts about their faith. Other preachers have come on the scene and confused the Galatians. Paul, frustrated with this setback, calls the Galatians "foolish," (Galatians 3:1). In another example, the way Paul reshapes the greeting tells us something about the purpose of the letter. In Paul's first letter to the Corinthians and in the letter to the Galatians, Paul begins the letter by mentioning his call as an apostle. He is subtly, or in the case of the Galatians, not so subtly, asserting his authority in dealing with the issues in these communities.

CONCLUSION

Anyone who studies Paul's letters and reads Luke's account of his missionary adventures will be stunned by the depth of Paul's love for Jesus Christ. At times he may appear irascible and argumentative, and at other times profound and compelling, but these tones convey only part of the measure of this man. He also had the enormous courage to reexamine his deeply held religious beliefs in his encounter with the risen Lord. He endured untold deprivations, traveling by foot across Asia Minor and Greece in a race against time, to share this stunning revelation of God's love for humanity in Christ Jesus. When people have a hard time understanding what Paul said, it might be helpful to step back and remember what Paul did and why.

Biblical scholars do not agree on the thirteen letters in the New Testament attributed to Paul. The letters below are listed in the order that Paul wrote them, though exact dates are hard to determine.

A. The Genuine Letters of Paul

Virtually all biblical scholars agree that these seven letters are from Paul himself:

1 Thessalonians	1 Corinthians
Galatians	2 Corinthians
Philippians	Romans
Philemon	

B. The Deutero-Pauline Letters

Scholars believe these letters were written while Paul was alive, but by a disciple of Paul:

2 Thessalonians
Colossians
Ephesians

C. The Pastoral Letters

These letters were written after Paul, by an unknown author who wanted to address new issues in the growing Christian communities with the authoritative voice of Paul:

Titus
1 Timothy
2 Timothy

QUESTIONS FOR DISCUSSSION

1. *Give three reasons why Paul was important in the first century of the Christian church.*
2. *Why is Acts of the Apostles less reliable for the story of Paul than Paul's own letters?*
3. *Using the seven undisputed letters of Paul, list the things that Paul tells us about himself. Arrange the information under three headings: a) before conversion, b) Paul's conversion experience, and c) after conversion.*
4. *Why do some biblical scholars believe the Pastoral Letters are not from Paul?*
5. *What can the form of a Pauline letter tell us about Paul or the community he addresses?*
6. *What is your favorite Pauline letter? Why?*

SUGGESTED READING

Cousar, Charles B. *The Letters of Paul* (Interpreting Biblical Texts series). Nashville, TN: Abingdon Press, 1996.

Murpy-O'Connor, Jerome. *Paul: His Story.* New York: Oxford University Press, 2006.

Sanders, E. P. Paul: *A Very Short Introduction.* New York: Oxford University Press, 2001.

Witherup, Ronald D. *101 Questions & Answers on Paul.* NY: Paulist Press, 2003.

CHAPTER 16

Reading the Book of Revelation Without "Going Off the Deep End"

ew books in the Bible have received such constant attention and interpretation as the Book of Revelation, and yet scholars and spiritual writers remain at odds on almost every important issue necessary for understanding this book. The purpose of this chapter is not to review the conflicting positions taken by biblical scholars over the centuries, but to suggest a path through this discussion that will help the ordinary reader make some sense out of a very difficult book without "going off the deep end."

WHAT KIND OF BOOK IS REVELATION?

The Book of Revelation is unique in the New Testament. It describes extraordinary visions most people never get to see. But in the time shortly before and after Christ (200 BCE–200 CE), such visions were not all that uncommon; the Book of Revelation was just one text in a much larger body of literature known as apocalyptic. It might be helpful to go back and read Chapter 11 of this book, "Is the End Near? Unraveling the Secrets of Apocalyptic Literature," for specific details about this kind of writing.

The book begins by telling us that it is "the revelation of Jesus Christ" (1:1). The Greek word for "revelation" is *apocalypsis,* from which comes our modern word "apocalyptic." People who read and study this kind of writing expect to find visions of the future filled with strange images, symbols, and mysterious words; that is the style of apocalyptic writing. But very quickly the book begins to sound like a letter of Saint Paul with a stylized greeting to seven churches in the Roman province of Asia (1:4–5), followed by seven separate messages (2—3), and concluding with the usual ending found in many New Testament letters (22:21). To make matters even more complicated, the author of the book refers to this work as "words of prophecy" (1:3) and returns to this theme in the final chapter of the book (22:7, 10, 18, 19). There are references to a group known as "the prophets" scattered throughout the book. Finally, the Book of Revelation is filled with beautiful, heavenly hymns that surely reflect some kind of connection to the liturgies that took place, many times in secret, in the homes of anxious believers.

So what kind of book is Revelation? Is it a letter or an apocalyptic vision? Is it a collection of prophetic sayings or a heavenly liturgy? How we answer these questions affects how we understand its content. Many people have concentrated on just one of these four types of literature; as a result they have an incomplete understanding of its powerful message. We must recognize and appreciate all four literary forms and the part they have played in shaping the message of this book.

Though some read Revelation with the expectation it will describe the sequence of events leading up to the final, fiery end, that approach is a serious misunderstanding of the purpose of apocalyptic writings. The author of these visions did not tell the faithful *how* or *when* the world would end, but rather assured those who were suffering for their faith that God would bring such evil to an end.

The book is also meant to be understood as a prophetic text. Here again there is confusion about what a prophetic text is supposed to do. Some people believe prophecy is meant to predict the future, and so they conclude that the book is describing the future and telling us how the final judgment of God will take place. But that approach is a misunderstanding of biblical prophecy. The purpose of a biblical prophet was to bring God's Word to a particular place and time, to prod that audience into reevaluating their choices and actions. The prophet may have spoken about future events, but those events were contingent upon decisions his audience made in response to God's Word at that moment. If they repented, the future would be different. The biblical prophets brought God's Word to the people, which required a response from those who heard it. Like the prophetic word of old, the words of prophecy in Revelation are God's Words, challenging the believer to look deeper into the present moment and reevaluate the decisions he or she is making now. Do not look for predictions about the future in it, but listen closely to what God is asking you to change in yourself right now.

The Book of Revelation is like a portal by which we get to peer into heaven. Again and again we encounter the apostles, martyrs, and saints worshipping the Lord God and the victorious Lamb. Their worship frequently erupts with hymns of praise. Though it is easy to discount these hymns in our interpretation of Revelation, they are a clue that the Book of Revelation was intended to be read in a worshipping community. Those hymns were most likely composed by unknown believers and sung in countless house churches throughout the Roman Empire. Like the familiar hymns sung in our churches today, they comforted and strengthened a faith under fire. The hymns were added to the heavenly liturgies by the author for a reason: to remind the early Christians how important it was to gather in worship and prayer. What they did is what the saints did in heaven. In times of suffering, these songs drove home an important message: to sing the hymns of Revelation is to believe that one does not sing or suffer alone!

Finally, "the revelation of Jesus Christ" (1:1), which technically begins in chapter four, is enveloped in the form of a letter. Elements of the letter form are found in chapters 1–3 and in the final chapter 22. In between those chapters, we find the apocalyptic visions and prophetic words. In the letters of Saint Paul, Paul wrote to specific communities to address practical problems they were facing in their faith journey. His words had a greater impact on the struggling community, because Paul wrote as the founder of that community. By wrapping this revelation in the form of a letter, the author did two things at once. First the letter form alerts us that the revelation was to be read aloud to the communities in a Roman province of Asia, and so we should pay close attention to the circumstances that existed in Roman Asia, and the communities of believers there. Secondly, just as any letter was meant to be understood by the recipient, so too the Book of Revelation was not intended to be a secret message, but one that the churches in this corner of Asia Minor would clearly understand. The Book of Revelation was never intended to be a secret to be unlocked in some distant future (Revelation 22:10). The book was meant to be understood by the audience that received it. When we understand what it said to them, we will be in a better position to hear what it says to our lives today.

WHEN WAS REVELATION WRITTEN AND BY WHOM?

A second set of interrelated issues revolves around when the book was written and by whom. Biblical scholars are divided on the date of the book: the more common opinion locates the book's appearance during the reign of the Roman emperor Domitian (81–96 CE). The other opinion places it earlier during the reign of Nero (54–68 CE). Because apocalyptic literature in general arises out of times of persecution, and because of the many references to the sufferings of the holy ones throughout the book, scholars look to either of these emperors because of the active persecution of Christians during their reigns. But there are problems with both of these timeframes. While the persecution of Christians by Nero is well documented, it was localized only to Rome and lasted a short time. The Book of Revelation is addressed to Christians living in a very different part of the Roman Empire. The persecution attributed to Domitian was more widespread and would have affected the Roman province of Asia, but reliable data that Domitian ordered such a general persecution of Christians is lacking. It does not mean that Christians did not suffer persecution, but new research suggests that the persecution at the end of the first century CE may have been more subtle, especially in the prosperous Roman province of Asia.

The book tells us that John is the author (1:1). But who is this John? The book calls him a "servant of God" (1:1) and a brother of those who are being addressed (1:9). At the end of the book, the revealing angel calls him a "fellow prophet" (22:9). These bits of information are not much to go on. It is clear, at least to scholars, that the John of Revelation is not the same John who wrote the Gospel. The grammar, style of writing, and vocabulary are significantly different in the two works. Since the book of Revelation never refers to him as an Apostle, it is better to think of him as an important figure to the Christians who lived in the Roman province of Asia.

THE PURPOSE AND PERSPECTIVE OF THE BOOK OF REVELATION

This book of visions was likely written to encourage Christians who were going through a time of severe persecution in the Roman Empire to remain steadfast in their faith. One not-so-subtle encouragement comes at the end of the book, where God and the Lamb remain standing, not the Beast! But since matching the Book of Revelation with the known periods of *active* persecution within the Roman Empire is difficult, scholars today have begun to examine the book in a new light.

The Book of Revelation employs several different literary

forms, giving it a unique perspective among the books of the New Testament. In the letters to the seven churches, we learn of some group(s) who were misleading the believers; they were called the "Nicolaitans" (2:14–15) and/or the prophetess Jezebel (2:20–23). Some scholars believe that spiritual leaders within the community argued for a more pragmatic approach for dealing with the pagan Roman culture. Instead of refusing to participate in the civic religious practices, such as acclaiming the emperor to be a god in a public assembly or throwing incense on an altar of the emperor at a political rally or eating meat from an animal sacrificed to one of the Roman gods, this group urged Christians to simply go along. It didn't really matter. Everyone knew that the emperor was not God. This was just political theatre; it was certainly not worth dying for. And in an economy that was raising the standard of living and visibility of many Christians in Roman Asia, they were beginning to have second thoughts about the necessity to publicly draw attention to their opposing beliefs. As long as they maintained their faith in private, why buck the culture that was raising their standard of living?

The argument made sense from a material perspective, but that was the problem. John saw this attitude as the newest threat to Christian faith and wrote his book to present an alternative perspective. In the very first vision (4:1), the author takes us up into heaven where we stay for the rest of the book. He wants us to see the world and its future from heaven's side, and it is quite an extraordinary view. Seen from heaven, things are not what they seem to be on earth.

The Book of Revelation is a prophetic warning, an urgent challenge to Christians to see behind the façade of the self-serving prosperity of the Roman Empire. From heaven one can see clearly the cost of keeping the empire afloat: the endless wars in the name of preserving security; the human misery of slavery that feeds a ravenous economy; the delusion of believing that a political institution was eternal when, in truth, it was just a thin veneer covering a beast dragging its followers into an endless ocean of fire. From heaven's side, as Revelation reveals, the "glory" of Rome was simply a painted whore lounging on the back of a bloodied, grotesque beast (Revelations 17).

CONCLUSION

The purpose of this powerful book was to bring those Christians back to their senses. The seven churches were called to be "lamp stands" for their communities (Revelations 1:12). John challenged his churches to see the beast just below the surface of the glitter and promise of their contemporary culture. Then Christians would see clearly the choices they had to make and the cost of their decisions. Seen from heaven, real power and glory are found in the Lamb that was sacrificed (Revelations 5:5–6). The Lamb was slain and the blood was real, and so the visions remind Christians of the terrifying cost of their choices. But the Book of Revelation is also a calming reassurance that if they (and we) can see behind the self-serving façade of one's own contemporary culture and compare it to the glory, purity, and endless beauty in the new city which is our real home (Revelations 21), then the choice is easy, even if the price is high.

DISCUSSION QUESTIONS

1. *What are the four different literary styles that are found in the Book of Revelation?*
2. *Which visions in the Book of Revelation made the most impression on you? Why?*
3. *Revelation 7 tells us that only one hundred forty-four thousand will be saved (twelve thousand from each of the twelve tribes of Israel). Is that true? How does that work in light of the staggering population explosion just within our own time?*

4. *How many different animals (real or mythical) can you find in the book of Revelation? What feelings do their descriptions evoke in you? Do you think the author deliberately did that?*
5. *If the book is not telling us when and how the world will end, then what is it trying to say?*
6. *Does the message of Revelation presented in this chapter have any application in your own life?*

FURTHER READING

Chapman, Charles T. *The Message of the Book of Revelation.* Collegeville, MN: Liturgical Press, 1995.

Faley, Roland J. *Apocalypse Then and Now: A Companion to the Book of Revelation.* New York: Paulist Press, 1999.

Harrington, Daniel J. *Revelation: The Book of the Risen Christ.* Hyde Park, NY: New City Press, 1999.

Schüssler Fiorenza, Elisabeth. *Revelation: Vision of a Just World* (Proclamation Commentaries). Minneapolis, MN: Fortress Press, 1991.

CHAPTER 17
The Gospels
the Church Left Behind

Did you know that Jesus never blinked and that he never left footprints when he walked? Did you know that when people touched Jesus, sometimes his flesh was warm and soft, and at other times it felt like a marble statue? You may not have heard these things, because none of them is found in the four Gospels of the New Testament. These descriptions come from other "gospels" and narratives that circulated among the early Christian communities of the second and third centuries CE. These documents are a small part of a much larger body of texts that were never accepted by the Church. They are the gospels the Church left behind.

The proper name for this larger collection of writings is *apocrypha*, which means "secret books." In literary form and style, these writings are similar to biblical books found in the Old and New Testaments, but the Christian churches never accepted them as inspired by God. It is important to remember that other types of writing were also in circulation among various Christian communities during those early years of the Church. There were "acts" of other apostles, letters of Paul and other apostles, and all kinds of apocalypses.

NEW TESTAMENT COUNTERPARTS

Among the apocrypha are various adventure narratives similar to the Acts of the Apostles, but these writings generally focus on the deeds of just one particular Apostle. For example, separate narratives tell of the acts of Andrew, John, Peter, Philip, and Thomas. Scholars today believe these types of narratives were popular because they were an early form of historical novel. Full of adventures and descriptions of foreign sites, they entertained their listeners. One of these narratives, the Acts of Paul and Thecla, contains several humorous stories about a young woman who fell in love with Paul and followed him from place to place, much to his chagrin. Other narratives are the source of some popularly held beliefs today. The Acts of Peter, for example, tells the story of how Peter was crucified upside down.

Besides various "acts," several letters were attributed to Saint Paul and other apostles. Among these letters is a third letter to the Corinthians, which dealt with several Gnostic heresies in the second century; clearly Paul did not write it. Another set of letters attributed to Paul was addressed to the Roman statesman Seneca (4 BCE–65 CE), a Stoic philosopher and contemporary of Paul, although there is no evidence that the two ever met. In the fourteen letters that make up this correspondence, Seneca admires Paul's talents and commends him to the emperor. Scholars believe that these fictitious letters were composed deliberately to give the already deceased Paul more standing in the estimation of the citizens of the Empire.

In the centuries before and after Christ, many apocalyptic books were produced; it was a period of great expectation for Jews, gentiles, and Christians. One of the more famous or infamous examples was the Apocalypse of Peter. In this writing, Peter was transported to heaven and given a tour of both hell and heaven similar to what Dante would describe many centuries later in his *Divine Comedy*. Like many such writings, the author's purpose is clearly evident, since the tour is more descriptive of the sufferings of hell than of the joys of heaven.

THE APOCRYPHAL GOSPELS

A number of gospels also circulated among the Christian communities during those early centuries. Several were supposedly written by other Apostles, such as Thomas, Peter, or Philip. In 2006, the Gospel of Judas grabbed national and international headlines. Scholars had known of its existence, because Saint Irenaeus quoted it in his five-volume work, *Against Heresies,* written in the second century to counteract the strong hold of Gnosticism in many Christian communities. Now scholars had a fragmentary manuscript containing the gospel in Coptic. It was a Gnostic document, as were many of the apocryphal gospels, which presented a decidedly different picture of Judas than that found in the four canonical Gospels. There was also a Gospel of Mary (Magdalene), the existence of which shows that she was held in high regard in some communities.

Some gospels, such as the Gospel of the Hebrews and the Gospel of the Egyptians, were attributed to an ethic group. Several infancy gospels, including the Protoevangelium of James and the Infancy Gospel of Thomas, dealt only with the early years of the child Jesus at home with Mary and Joseph. Several of the apocryphal gospels are simply long, complex dialogues which resemble the dialogues found in the Gospel of John, but have no context or setting. The Gospel of the Four Heavenly Regions, the Gospel of Truth, and the Dialogue of the Redeemer are just a few of these gospel discourses.

The church rejected and suppressed the apocryphal gospels for many reasons, but hiding or covering up some terrible secret was not one of them. Today people are more suspicious of authority, especially when it is a "church" authority, and are ready to believe in diabolic plots to keep the "real truth" hidden from believers. That is the stuff of fiction. If a person were to read some of these gospels, it would become very clear in a very short time why some of them never made it into the New Testament.

Many of these gospels contained pious legends that were meant to edify a particular audience, but over time these stories came to be regarded as rather silly. The Infancy Gospel of Thomas is a good example of this kind of collection. It contained stories about Jesus as a pre-teen; apparently the author wanted to show how Jesus' character developed during this period of time.

The gospel portrayed Jesus at first as a rather immature child who used his powers only for his own advantage; in many cases the townspeople were terrified of him. In time he learned to use his powers for the good of others, and their attitudes began to change. The gospel described one incident in which Jesus was making birds out of clay on the Sabbath. When a neighbor reported this to Joseph, Jesus brought the clay birds to life and they promptly flew away, leaving no evidence that he had broken the Sabbath. In another incident Jesus was helping Joseph make a bed for a customer. But when Joseph realized the two main planks for the bed were not the same length Jesus laid them side by side and pulled on the shorter plank until it stretched to match the longer one.

FILLING IN THE GAPS IN THE LIFE OF JESUS

In some cases the apocryphal gospels tried to fill in the gaps of the canonical Gospels; still the Church authorities rejected them because they created more problems than they solved. In the Protoevangelium of James, an infancy gospel attributed to James, we are told about Mary's birth and her early years before she was engaged to Joseph. This kind of detail is just what modern readers want to know, but when the story is told, we are left with many problems. In what sounds like "déjà vu" (think of the story of Hannah and Elkanah in the first Book of Samuel 1 or the story of Elizabeth and Zechariah in Luke 1), Anne and Joachim found themselves humiliated because they were childless. The situation changed dramatically when an angel of the Lord visited Anne with the news that she would have a child.

When Mary was born, the couple was so overjoyed, they vowed to take her to Jerusalem on her second birthday and let her be raised by the priests in the Temple. But the approach of Mary's second birthday made Anne so sad that Joachim suggested a one-year delay. On her third birthday, Mary's parents brought her to the Temple. This is a beautiful story, but its similarity to other biblical narratives leaves one with the sense that the story was contrived to show that Mary's birth was similar to other famous biblical figures: Samuel and John the Baptist.

FALSE TEACHINGS

The primary reason that many of these gospels were suppressed was that they simply contained false teachings either about Jesus or attributed to him. We have to remember that it took almost three hundred years before the Church had a creed outlining the basic elements of Christian belief. In the meantime, there were many attempts to grapple with the mystery of how Jesus was both human and divine. Some explanations were popular and had a large following; others were taught in smaller locales. Bishops learned about these various teachings, which often circulated in the form of a gospel, and they wrote letters to correct the errors. They also tried to suppress these gospels to prevent the spread of erroneous teachings.

The existing portion of the Gospel of Peter revealed a number of differences with the accounts in the New Testament. In this gospel, Pilate left the fate of Jesus with Herod, who then decided to have Jesus crucified. It was clear Herod was in charge, because when Joseph of Arimathea asked Pilate for the body of Jesus after his death, Pilate had to ask Herod for that permission. (Here we see a theme that would continue to reappear: the absolution of Pilate and the indiscriminate condemnation of the Jews for Jesus' death.)

Other differences in this account are even more puzzling. The soldiers, for example, nailed Jesus to the cross only by his hands, not his feet. The Gospel of Peter went on to say that Jesus remained silent throughout the ordeal "as if he was in no pain" (4:1). This sentence troubled church authorities, because it gave the erroneous impression that Jesus did not suffer in his crucifixion. The gospel subtly says that Jesus really was not human, just divine.

In other gospels, Jesus teaches heresy. In the Gospel of Mary, for example, the risen Jesus, his Apostles, and Mary Magdalene were discussing several issues. Peter asked Jesus about sin, and he replied that there was no such thing as sin! This shocking statement, placed on the lips of Jesus, represented a common Gnostic belief. Many of the apocryphal gospels used Jesus to teach their Gnostic beliefs. The Gospel of Thomas is one of the best examples.

The Gospel of Thomas, like the Gospel of Philip, is not really a gospel at all. Rather, it is a collection of one hundred fourteen sayings attributed to Jesus. Many of the sayings are very similar to ones found in the canonical Gospels. Others sound similar, but are just different enough to confuse. For example, Jesus says: "Let him who seeks continue seeking until he finds. When he finds, he will become troubled. When he becomes troubled, he will be astonished, and he will rule over the All" (Gospel of Thomas, 2). Many of the sayings are intentionally mysterious: "That which you have will save you if you bring it forth from yourselves. That which you do not have within you will kill you if you do not have it within you" (Gospel of Thomas, 70). Because Gnosticism was so prevalent throughout the Roman Empire, any gospel texts reflecting this heresy were vehemently condemned, and if possible, the texts were destroyed.

CONCLUSION

Since the publication of Dan Brown's *The Da Vinci Code*, millions of readers have found themselves intrigued by the idea of hidden writings supposedly suppressed by the early church because of the secrets they contained. In truth, many apocryphal writings were set aside as the early church came to better understand the teachings of Jesus and the meaning of his death and resurrection. But these documents are certainly not secret. Popular bookstores and university libraries offer modern translations of these ancient texts for anyone to read.

What possible value might these texts have if the church has rejected them as false? They give us a better picture of the first few centuries after Christ and how Christian communities all around the Mediterranean came to understand what Jesus said and meant. It was a confusing time, at best. These texts also help us learn how the Jesus tradition grew and developed in those early decades after his death and resurrection. Scholars have long argued that there must have been a collection of sayings of Jesus that Matthew and Luke used in composing their Gospels. The existence of the apocryphal Gospel of Thomas, though much later than the four canonical Gospels, is an example of just such a collection, making it possible that an authentic collection of Jesus' words did exist at one time. We can now better understand how, in the heat and confusion of those first three centuries, a great many texts tried to shape Christian beliefs about Jesus. In the end, they simply became the gospels the church left behind.

DISCUSSION QUESTIONS

1. *Why are the books discussed in this chapter called "apocrypha"?*
2. *Are these writings considered false?*
3. *What does the Gospel of Judas say about Judas and Jesus? (If possible, go to the National Geographic website and read a summary of the gospel: http://www.nationalgeographic. com/lostgospel/.)*
4. *Why aren't these apocryphal gospels helpful in filling the blanks that are found in the four New Testament Gospels?*
5. *What is the value of the Gospel of Thomas for people who study the Gospels? Should Christians be reading these books if they were not included in the Bible?*

FURTHER READING

Ehrman, Bart D. *Lost Christianities: The Battles for Scripture and the Faiths We Never Knew.* New York: Oxford University Press, 2003.

Ehrman, Bart D. *Lost Scriptures: Books That Did Not Make It Into the New Testament.* New York: Oxford University Press, 2005.

Lapham, F. *An Introduction to the New Testament Apocrypha.* New York: T&T Clark International, 2003.

Perkins, Pheme. *Gnosticism and the New Testament.* Minneapolis: Fortress Press, 1993.

The Apocryphal New Testament: A Collection of Apocryphal Christian Literature in an English Translation. Elliott, J. K., ed. New York: Oxford University Press, 1993.